DISCARDED

The Indians
of the
Pike's Peak Region

PISCHEL YEARBOOKS, INC.
P. O. Box 36 Marceline, Missouri 64658
Telephone (816) 376-3523

The Indians
of the
Pike's Peak Region,

Including an Account of the Battle of Sand Creek, and of Occurrences in El Paso County, Colorado, during the War with the Cheyennes and Arapahoes, in 1864 and 1868

By

Irving Howbert

Illustrated

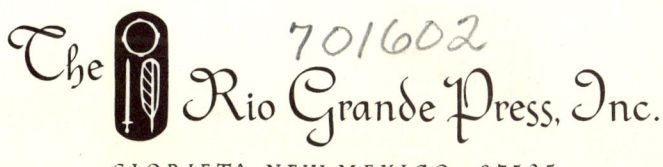

The Rio Grande Press, Inc.

GLORIETA, NEW MEXICO · 87535

First edition from which this edition
was reproduced was supplied by
FRED ROSENSTOCK, Books
1228 East Colfax Avenue
Denver, Colo. 80218

A RIO GRANDE CLASSIC
First published in 1914

LIBRARY OF CONGRESS CARD CATALOG 76-119861
I.S.B.N. 87380-045-1

First Printing 1970

GLORIETA, NEW MEXICO · 87535

Publisher's Preface

The two books written by the late Irving Howbert (this one in 1914 and *Memories of a Lifetime in the Pike's Peak Region* in 1925) were brought to our attention first by our friend and colleague in Corpus Christi, Tex., Louis V. Boling, Bookseller. Mr. Boling wrote and suggested we publish the other title, and sent us his first edition with which to work. We wrote to our friend at the beautiful Penrose Public Library in Colorado Springs, Librarian Margaret Reid, to invite her opinion. She recommended we publish the other title, and this one, too. So, once again, they are both back in print--considerably improved in format. The first edition did not have an index; we had one prepared by our friend Katherine McMahon of Albuquerque, N.M., and it is included at the back of this book. We also have added a Territorial map of Colorado, a negative therefor being obtained from the splendid Western History Collection of the Denver Public Library--thanks to librarian Alys Freeze.

We added something else, too, which we conceive to be very special. That is the wonderful foldout print of the Indians, c. 1913. This picture was taken by Clarence Coil, of Colorado Springs. The original print hangs over the door in the office of Mr. Floyd Brunson, operator of Stewarts Commercial Photographers, Inc. We were working closely with the staff of the First National Bank of Colorado Springs, and Vice President Gordon Culver sent us over to see Mr. Brunson about a picture of the bank (founded in 1874 by the author of this book). The first thing we saw in Mr. Brunson's office was this beautiful photograph of Ute Indians taken at about the time this book was written.

Mr. Brunson was as courteous and cooperative as he could be, and yes, he would permit us to use the photograph in the book. In the due course of time we received a negative of the print, on loan, and with it an identification of one kind or another for all the people in the picture. Note caption of the foldout. When the picture was taken, c. 1913, most of the people in the lineup were well known to the citizens of the Pike's Peak region. While this photograph is not particulary germane to the text of this book, it is very germane to the time the book was written. Moreover, scenes like the one pictured do not occur any more except around a movie studio. This picture is completely authentic, and hence, we think, of interest to any reader of this book.

The Penrose Public Library had no copy of this title, but our good friend Fred Rosenstock in Denver did. Mr. Rosenstock and his wife Frances sells rare books and paintings at their handsome store in Denver. Few men we know are as knowledgeable about rare books as Fred Rosenstock. Besides being an unquestioned authority on rare books, he is himself a publisher. He publishes fine editions from time to time under the colophon of the Old West Publishing Co. Fred and Frances are simply wonderful people. We have received their active help and encouragement ever since we founded The Rio Grande Press. We are mighty pleased to count them both as our friends.

When in the course of reading this book and the other Howbert title, we discovered that the author not only was a principle founder of Colorado Springs, but he also was a founder of the city's First National Bank and served twice as its president. The Howbert family and tradition of public service survives still in that lovely city, as the author's grandson, also Irving Howbert, is a prominent attorney still active in civic affairs. He is at this time, also a member of the board of directors of the bank. Mr. Howbert was delighted to learn we were reprinting the books, and he and the staff of the bank (especially Vice President Gordon Culver) extended us every possible help they could.

In a project like this, one would be remiss in not calling on a Chamber of Commerce, where always reposes a bountiful supply of pictures and cooperative people. We therefore called on the Colorado Springs C. of C. With the help of fetching Mrs. Nancy J. Hascall (executive secretary), we were able to procure most of the rare old pictures we used in the folio at the back of *Memories of a Lifetime in the Pike's Peak Region* If a reader likes this book, he is bound to like that one, too.

This title is the 64th in our series of beautiful Rio Grande Classics, and *Memories of a Lifetime in the Pike's Peak Region* is our 63rd. These numbers are merely chronological in the series, and have no particular relevance except for those who like to keep count... us, mainly. There is no historic significance to our numbering system. We started with No. 1 in 1962, and eight years later we publish No. 63 and No. 64. We only wish that our fine books were in as much demand when they are in print as they are when they go out of print.

Robert B. McCoy

La Casa Escuela
Glorieta, N. M.
October 1970

Pike's Peak

From a painting by Charles Craig

The Indians
of the
Pike's Peak Region

Including an Account of the Battle of Sand
Creek, and of Occurrences in El Paso
County, Colorado, during the War
with the Cheyennes and Arapahoes, in 1864 and 1868

By

Irving Howbert

Illustrated

The Knickerbocker Press
New York
1914

COPYRIGHT, 1914
BY
IRVING HOWBERT

CONTENTS

	PAGE
THE TRIBES OF THE PIKE'S PEAK REGION	1
TRAILS, MINERAL SPRINGS, GAME, ETC.	27
THE INDIAN TROUBLES OF 1864	75
THE THIRD COLORADO AND THE BATTLE OF SAND CREEK	93
A DEFENSE OF THE BATTLE OF SAND CREEK	114
A DEFENSE OF THE BATTLE OF SAND CREEK—CONTINUED	147
THE INDIAN WAR OF 1868	187

ILLUSTRATIONS

	FACING PAGE
PIKE'S PEAK	*Frontispiece*
OURAY	60
COLONEL JOHN M. CHIVINGTON	117
GOVERNOR JOHN EVANS	123

INTRODUCTION

FOR the most part this book is intentionally local in its character. As its title implies, it relates principally to the Indian tribes that have occupied the region around Pike's Peak during historic times.

The history, habits, and customs of the American Indian have always been interesting subjects to me. From early childhood, I read everything within my reach dealing with the various tribes of the United States and Mexico. In 1860, when I was fourteen years of age, I crossed the plains between the Missouri River and the Rocky Mountains twice, and again in 1861, 1865, and 1866; each time by ox- or horse-team, there being no other means of conveyance. At that time there were few railroads west of the Mississippi River and none west of the Missouri. On each of these trips I came more or less into contact with the Indians, and during my residence in Colorado from 1860 to the present time, by observation and by study, I have become more or less familiar with all the tribes of this Western country.

From 1864 to 1868, the Indians of the plains were hostile to the whites; this resulted in many tragic happenings in that part of the Pike's Peak region embracing El Paso and its adjoining counties, as well as elsewhere in the Territory of Colorado. I then lived in Colorado City, in El Paso County, and took an active part in the defense of the settlements during all the Indian troubles in that section. I mention these facts merely to show that I am not unfamiliar with the subject about which I am writing. My main object in publishing this book is to make a permanent record of the principal events of that time.

So far as I know, the public has never been given a detailed account of the Indian troubles in El Paso County during the years 1864 and 1868. At that time there was no newspaper published in the county and the few newspapers of the Territory were small affairs, in which little attention was given to anything outside of their immediate localities. The result was that news of tragic happenings in our part of the Territory seldom passed beyond the borders of our own county.

I have thought best to begin with a short account of the tribes occupying the Pike's Peak

Introduction

region prior to the coming of the white settler, adding to it extracts from the descriptions given by early explorers, together with an account of the game, trails, etc., of this region. All these facts will no doubt be of interest to the inhabitant of the present day, as well as of value to the future historian.

I took part in the battle of Sand Creek, and in many of the other events which I mention. Where I have no personal knowledge of any particular event, I have taken great pains to obtain the actual facts by a comparison of the statements of persons who I knew lived in the locality at the time. Consequently, I feel assured of the substantial accuracy of every account I have given.

In giving so much space to a defense of the battle of Sand Creek, I am impelled by an earnest desire to correct the false impression that has gone forth concerning that much maligned affair. Statements of prejudiced and unreliable witnesses concerning the battle were sent broadcast at the time, but except through government reports, that only few read, never before, to my knowledge, has publicity been given to the statement of the Governor of the Territory, telling of the conditions leading up to the battle, or to the sworn testimony of the colonel in command at the engagement, or of the officer in command of the fort near which it was fought. That the battle of Sand Creek was not the reprehensible affair which vindictive persons have represented it to be, I believe is conclusively proven by the evidence which I present.

I. H.

COLORADO SPRINGS,
November 1, 1913.

The Indians of the Pike's Peak Region

CHAPTER I

THE TRIBES OF THE PIKE'S PEAK REGION

IT would be interesting to know who were the occupants of the Pike's Peak region during prehistoric times. Were its inhabitants always nomadic Indians? We know that semi-civilized peoples inhabited southwestern Colorado and New Mexico in prehistoric times, who undoubtedly had lived there ages before they were driven into cliff dwellings and communal houses by savage invaders. Did their frontier settlements of that period ever extend into the Pike's Peak region? The facts concerning these matters, we may never know. As it is, the earliest definite information we have concerning the occupants of this region dates from the Spanish exploring expeditions, but even that is very meager. From this and other sources, we know that a succession of Indian tribes moved southward along the eastern base of the Rocky Mountains during the two hundred years before the coming of the white settler, and that during this period, the principal tribes occupying this region were the Utes, Comanches, Kiowas, Cheyennes, Arapahoes, and Sioux; and, further, that there were other tribes such as the Pawnees and Jicarilla Apaches, who frequently visited and hunted in this region.

The Jicarilla Apaches are of the Athapascan stock, a widely distributed linguistic family, which includes among its branches the Navajos, the Mescalaros of New Mexico, and the Apaches of Arizona. Notwithstanding the fact that they were kindred people, the Jicarillas considered the latter tribes their enemies. However, they always maintained friendly relations with the Utes, and the Pueblos of northern New Mexico, and intermarriages between members of these tribes were of frequent occurrence. The mother of Ouray, the noted Ute chief, was a Jicarilla Apache.

From the earliest period, the principal home of the Jicarilla Apaches was along the Rio Grande

River in northern New Mexico, but in their wanderings they often went north of the Arkansas River and far out on the plains, where they had an outpost known as the Quartelejo. By reason of the intimate relations existing between the Jicarillas and the Pueblo Indians, this outpost was more than once used as a place of refuge by members of the latter tribes. Bancroft, in his history of New Mexico, says that certain families of Taos Indians went out into the plains about the middle of the seventeenth century and fortified a place called "Cuartalejo," which undoubtedly is but another spelling of the name Quartelejo. These people remained at Quartelejo for many years, but finally returned to Taos at the solicitation of an agent sent out by the Government of New Mexico. In 1704, the Picuris, another Pueblo tribe, whose home was about forty miles north of Sante Fé, abandoned their village in a body and fled to Quartelejo, but they also returned to New Mexico two years later. Quartelejo is frequently mentioned in the history of New Mexico, and its location is described as being 130 leagues northeast of Santa Fé. In recent years the ruin of a typical Pueblo structure has been unearthed on Beaver Creek in Scott County, Kansas, about two hundred miles east of Colorado Springs, which, in direction and distance from Santa Fé, coincides with the description given of Quartelejo, and is generally believed to be that place.

Aside from the Jicarilla Apaches, the Utes, living in the mountainous portion of the region now included in the State of Colorado, were the earliest occupants of whom there is any historical account. They were mentioned in the Spanish records of New Mexico as already inhabiting the region to the north of that Territory in the early part of the seventeenth century. At that time, and for many years afterward, they were on peaceable terms with the Spanish settlers of New Mexico. About 1705, however, something occurred to disturb their friendly relations, and a war resulted which lasted fifteen to twenty years, during which time many people were killed, numerous ranches were plundered, and many horses stolen. Although the Utes already owned many horses, it is said that in these raids they acquired so many more that they were able to mount their entire tribe. During that time various military expeditions were sent against the Utes as well as against the Comanches, who had first appeared in New Mexico in 1716. In 1719, the Governor of New Mexico led a military force, consisting of 105 Spaniards and a large number of Indian auxiliaries,

The Pike's Peak Region

into the region which is now the State of Colorado, against the hostile bands. The record of the expedition says that it left Santa Fé on September 15th and marched north, with the mountains on the left, until October 10th. In this twenty-five days' march the expedition should have gone far beyond the place where Colorado Springs now stands. Although the expedition failed to overtake the Indians, the latter ceased their raids for a time, but their subsequent outbreaks showed that their friendship for the New Mexican people could not be entirely depended upon, although they mingled with them to such an extent that a large portion of the tribe acquired a fair knowledge of the Spanish language.

The Utes were an offshoot of the Shoshone family, the branches of which have been widely distributed over the Rocky Mountain region from the Canadian line south into Mexico. It is now generally conceded that the Aztecs of Mexico and the Utes belong to the same linguistic family. It is probable that in the march of the former toward the south, many centuries ago, the Utes were left behind, remaining in their savage state, while the Aztecs, coming in contact with the semi-civilized nations of the South, gradually reached the state of culture which they had attained at the time of the conquest of Mexico by the Spaniards. I am firmly of the opinion that these Indians, and in fact all the Indians of America, are descendants of Asiatic tribes that crossed over to this continent by way of Bering Strait at some remote period. These tribes may, however, have been added to at various times by chance migrations from Japan, the Hawaiian and South Sea islands. It is known that in historic times the Japanese current has thrown upon the Pacific Coast fishing-boats, laden with Japanese people, which had drifted helplessly across the Pacific Ocean. It is, therefore, fair to assume that what is known to have occurred in recent times might also have frequently occurred in the remote past, and if this be so, the intermarriage of these people with the native races would undoubtedly have had a decided influence upon the tribes adjacent to the Pacific Coast. There seems to be no reason why the people of the Hawaiian Islands should not have visited our shores, as those islands are not much farther distant from the Pacific Coast than are certain inhabited islands in other directions. These same conclusions have been reached by many others who have made a study of the question.

The *National Geographic Magazine* of April,

1910, contained an article written by Miss Scidmore on "Mukden, the Manchu Home," in which she says:

When I saw the Viceroy and his suite at a Japanese fête at Tairen, whither he had gone to pay a state visit, I was convinced as never before of the common origin of the North American Indian and the Chinese or Manchu Tartars. There before me might as well have been Red Cloud, Sitting Bull, and Rain-in-the-Face, dressed in blue satin blankets, thick-soled moccasins, and squat war-bonnets with single bunches of feathers shooting back from the crown. Manchu eyes, Tartar cheek-bones, and Mongol jaws were combined in countenances that any Sioux chief would recognize as a brother.

The Ute Indians were well-built, but not nearly as tall as the Sioux, Cheyennes, Arapahoes, or any of the tribes of the plains. Their type of countenance was substantially the same as that of all American Indians. They were distinctly mountain Indians, and that they should have been a shorter race than those of the plains to the east is peculiar, as it reverses the usual rule. Might not this have been the result of an infusion of Japanese blood in the early days of the Shoshones when their numbers were small? And possibly from this same source came the unusual ability of the Utes in warfare.

As Indians go, the Utes were a fairly intelligent people. They had a less vicious look than the Indians of the plains, and as far as my observation goes, they were not so cruel. They ranged over the mountainous region from the northern boundaries of the present State of Colorado, down as far as the central part of New Mexico. Their favorite camping-place, however, was in the beautiful valleys of the South Park, and other places in the region west of Pike's Peak. The South Park was known to the old trappers and hunters as the Bayou Salado, probably deriving its name from the salt marshes and springs that were abundant in the western part of that locality.

Game was to be found in greater abundance in the South Park and the country round about than in almost any other region of the Rocky Mountains, and for that reason its possession was contended for most strenuously year after year by all the tribes of the surrounding country. For a time in the summer season, the Utes were frequently driven away from this favorite region by the tribes of the plains who congregated in the South Park in great numbers as soon as the heat of the plains became uncomfortable. However, the Utes seldom failed to retain possession during most of the year, as they were remarkably good fighters and more than able to hold their own against equal numbers.

In point of time, the Comanches were the next tribe of which we have any record, as inhabiting this region. These Indians also were a branch of the Shoshone nation. They led the procession of tribes that moved southward along the eastern base of the Rocky Mountains during the seventeenth and the first half of the eighteenth centuries. When first heard of, they were occupying the territory where the Missouri River emerges from the Rocky Mountains. Later, they were driven south by the pressure of the Sioux Indians and other tribes coming in from the north and east. For a while they occupied the Black Hills, and then were pushed still farther south by the Kiowas. They joined their kinsmen the Utes in raids upon the settlements of New Mexico in 1716, and it was to punish the Comanches as well as the Utes, that the Governor of New Mexico, in 1719, led the military expedition into the country now within the boundaries of Colorado. In 1724, Bourgemont, a French explorer mentions them under the name of the Padouca, as located between the headwaters of the Platte and Kansas rivers, but later accounts show that before the end of that century they had been pushed south of the

Arkansas River by the pressure of the tribes to the north.

During the stay of the Comanches in this region, they were for a time friendly with the Utes, and the two tribes joined each other in warfare and roamed over much of the same territory, but later, for some unknown reason, they for a time engaged in a deadly warfare. The old legend of the Manitou Springs mentions the possible beginning of the trouble. The incident around which the legend is woven, may be an imaginary one, but it is a well-known fact that long and bitter wars between tribes resulted from slighter causes. It is said that a long war between the Delawares and Shawnees originated in a quarrel between two children over a grasshopper.

The Comanches were a nation of daring warriors, and after their removal to the south of the Arkansas River, they became a great scourge to the settlements of Texas and New Mexico, finally extending their raids as far as Chihuahua, in Mexico. As a result of these operations, they became rich in horses and plunder obtained in their raids, besides securing as captives many American and Spanish women and children. One of their most noted chiefs in after days was the son of a white woman who had been captured in Texas in her childhood, and who, when grown, had married a Comanche chief. The Government arranged for the release of both the American and Spanish captives, but in more than one instance women who had been captured in their younger days refused to leave their Comanche husbands, notwithstanding the strongest urging on the part of their own parents.

Following the Comanches came the Kiowas, a tribe of unknown origin, as their language seems to have no similarity to that of any of the other tribes of this country. According to their mythology, their first progenitors emerged from a hollow cottonwood log, at the bidding of a supernatural ancestor. They came out one at a time as he tapped upon the log, until it came to the turn of a fleshy woman, who stuck fast in the hole, and thus blocked the way for those behind her, so that they were unable to follow. This, they say, accounts for the small number of the Kiowa tribe.

The first mention of this tribe locates them at the extreme sources of the Yellowstone and Missouri rivers, in what is now central Montana. Later, by permission of the Crow Indians, they took up their residence east of that tribe and became allied with them. Up to this time they possessed no horses and in moving about had to depend solely upon dogs. They finally drifted out upon the plains; here they first procured horses, and came in contact with the Arapahoes, Cheyennes, and, later, with the Sioux. The tribe probably secured horses by raids upon the Spaniards of New Mexico, as the authorities of that Territory mention the Kiowas as early as 1748, while the latter were still living in the Black Hills. It may not be generally known that there were no horses upon the American continent prior to the coming of the Spaniards. The first horses acquired by the Indians were those lost or abandoned by the early exploring expeditions, and these were added to later by raids upon the Spanish settlements of New Mexico. The natural increase of the horses so obtained gave the Indians, in many cases, a number in excess of their needs. Previous to acquiring horses, the Indians used dogs in moving their belongings around the country. As compared with their swift movements of later days this slow method of transportation very materially limited their migrations.

By the end of that century, the Kiowas had drifted south into the region embraced by the present State of Colorado, probably being forced to do so by the pressure of the Sioux, Cheyennes, and Arapahoes, who were at that time advancing from the north and east. As the Kiowas advanced southward, they encountered the Comanches; this resulted in warfare that lasted many years, in the course of which the Comanches were gradually driven south of the Arkansas River. When, finally, the war was terminated, an alliance was effected between the two tribes, which thereafter remained unbroken. In 1806, the Kiowas were occupying the country along the eastern base of the mountains of the Pike's Peak region. From Lieut. Zebulon Pike's narrative, we learn that James Pursley, who, according to Lieutenant Pike, was the first American to penetrate the immense wilds of Louisiana, spent a trading season with the Kiowas and Comanches in 1802 and 1803. He remained with them until the next spring, when the Sioux drove them from the plains into the mountains at the head of the Platte and Arkansas rivers. In all probability their retreat into the mountains was through Ute Pass, as that was the most accessible route. In the same statement Lieutenant Pike mentions Pursley's claim to having found gold on the headwaters of the Platte River. By the year 1815, most of the Kiowas had been pushed south of the Arkansas River by the Cheyennes and Arapahoes, but not until 1840 did they finally give up fighting for the possession of this region.

The Cheyennes and Arapahoes were of the Algonquin linguistic family, whose original home was in the New England States and southern Canada. When first heard of, about 1750, the Cheyennes were located in northern Minnesota. Later, about 1790, they were living on the Missouri, near the mouth of the Cheyenne River. Subsequently they moved west into the Black Hills, being forced to do so by the enmity of the Sioux. Here they were joined by the Arapahoes, a tribe of the same Algonquin stock, and from that time on the two tribes were bound together in the closest relations.

Beginning about 1800, these two federated tribes, accompanied by some of the Sioux, with whom they had made peace, gradually moved southward along the eastern base of the Rocky Mountains. Dr. James, the historian of Long's expedition which visited the Pike's Peak region in 1820, mentions the fact that about four years previous there had been a large encampment of Indians on a stream near Platte Cañon, southwest of Denver, which had assembled for trading purposes. It appears that the Cheyennes had been supplied with goods by British traders on the Missouri River, and had met to exchange these goods for horses. The tribes dwelling on the fertile plains of the Arkansas and Red rivers always had a great number of horses, which they reared with much less difficulty than did the Cheyennes, who usually spent the winter in the country farther to the north, where the cold weather lasted much longer and feed was less abundant. After many years of warfare with the Kiowas, the Cheyennes and Arapahoes were victorious, and by a treaty, made in 1840, secured undisputed possession of the territory north of the Arkansas River and east of the mountains. As this was only eighteen years before the coming of the whites, the Cheyennes and Arapahoes could not rightfully claim this region as their ancestral home. The country acquired by the Cheyennes and Arapahoes, through their victory over the Kiowas, embraced a territory of more than eighty thousand square miles. As in those two tribes there were never more than five thousand men, women, and children, all told, the area was out of all proportion to their numbers.

Early in 1861, the Government made a treaty with the Cheyennes and Arapahoes by which these tribes gave up the greater part of the lands claimed by them in the new Territory of Colorado. For this they were to receive a consideration of four hundred and fifty thousand dollars, to be paid in fifteen yearly installments, the tribes reserving for their own use a tract about seventy miles square located on both sides of the Arkansas River in the southeastern part of the Territory.

From the time of their first contact with the whites, the Cheyennes and Arapahoes were alternately friendly or hostile, just as their temper or whim dictated upon any particular occasion. With the old trappers and hunters of the plains, the Cheyennes had the reputation of being the most treacherous and untrustworthy at all times and in all places, of any of the tribes of the West. The Arapahoes, while occasionally committing depredations against the whites, were said to be somewhat different in temperament, in that they were not so sullen and morose as the Cheyennes, and were less treacherous and more open and trustworthy in their dealings. This estimate of the characteristics of the two tribes was fully confirmed in our contact with them in the early days of Colorado.

The Cheyennes were continuously hostile during the years 1855, 1856, and 1857, killing many whites and robbing numerous wagon-trains along the Platte River, which at that time was the great thoroughfare for travelers to Utah, California, Oregon, and other regions to the west of the Rocky Mountains. In 1857, the Cheyennes were severely punished in a number of engagements by troops under command of Colonel E. V. Sumner of the regular army, and as a result, they gave little trouble during the next five or six years.

In the early days, the Arapahoes came in touch with the whites to a much greater extent than did the Cheyennes. The members of the latter tribe usually held aloof, and by their manner plainly expressed hatred of the white race. Horace Greeley, in his book describing his trip across the plains to California in 1859, tells of a large body of Arapahoes who were encamped on the outskirts of Denver in June of that year, because of the protection they thought it gave them from their enemies the Utes. I saw this band when I passed through Denver in June of the following year.

The Sioux were one of the largest Indian nations upon the American continent. So far as is known, their original home was upon the Atlantic Coast in North Carolina, but by the time Europeans began to settle in that section they had drifted into the Western country. Their first contact with the white race occurred in the upper Mississippi region. These white people were the French explorers who had penetrated into almost every part of the interior long before the English had made any serious attempt at the exploration of the wilderness west of the Allegheny Mountains. The friendly relations between the French and the Sioux continued for many years, but when the French were finally supplanted by the English in most localities, the Sioux made an alliance with the latter which was maintained during the Revolutionary War, and continued until after the War of 1812. Subsequent to the year 1812, the Sioux gradually drifted still farther westward, and not many years later their principal home was upon the upper Missouri River. The recognized southern boundary of their country was the North Platte River, but on account of their friendly relations with the Cheyennes and Arapahoes, the Sioux often wandered along the base of the mountains as far as the Arkansas River, and, being at enmity with the Utes, they frequently joined the Cheyennes and Arapahoes in raids upon their common enemy.

While the Pawnees seldom spent much time in this region, they often came to the mountains in raids upon their enemies the Sioux, Cheyennes, Arapahoes, and Kiowas and upon horse-stealing expeditions. The Pawnees were members of the Caddoan family, whose original home was in the South. In this they were exceptional, since almost every other tribe in this Western country came from the north or east. From time immemorial their principal villages were located on the Loup Fork of the Platte River and on the headwaters of the Republican River, about three hundred miles east of the Rocky Mountains. The Pawnees were a warlike tribe and extended their raids over a very wide stretch of country, at times reaching as far as New Mexico. They carried on a bitter warfare with the Sioux, Cheyennes, and Arapahoes, and at times were engaged in warfare with almost every one of the surrounding tribes. They were a courageous people, and were generally victorious, where the numbers engaged were at all nearly equal. The Spaniards of New Mexico became acquainted with this tribe as early as 1693, and made strenuous efforts to maintain friendly relations with them; with few exceptions these efforts were successful.

In 1720, the Spanish authorities of New Mexico learned that French traders had established trading stations in the Pawnee country, and were furnishing the Indians with firearms. This news greatly disturbed the Spaniards and resulted in a military expedition being organized at Santa Fé, to visit the principal villages of the Pawnees for the purpose of impressing that tribe with the strength of the Spanish Government, and thus to counteract the influence of the French. The expedition started from Santa Fé in June of that year. It was under the command of Lieutenant-Colonel Villazur, of the Spanish regular army, and was composed of fifty armed Spaniards, together with a large number of Jicarilla Apache Indians as auxiliaries, making the expedition an imposing one for the times. The route taken, as nearly as I can determine from the description given in Bancroft's history of New Mexico, was northerly along the eastern base of the mountains, passing not very far from where Colorado Springs is now located. After reaching the Platte River, at no great distance east of the mountains, the expedition proceeded down the valley of that stream until it came in contact with the Pawnees, but before a council could be held, the latter surprised the Spaniards, killed the commanding officer, and in the fight that ensued almost annihilated the party. The surviving half-dozen soldiers, who were mounted, saved themselves by flight. Not yet having acquired horses, the Pawnees could not pursue them. These survivors, after untold hardships, reached Santa Fé a month or two later to tell the tale. Another instance of a Spanish force visiting the Pawnees occurred in 1806. When Lieutenant Pike on his exploring tour visited

The Pike's Peak Region

the Pawnees on the Republican River in September of that year, he found that a Spanish military force had been there just ahead of him. This force had been dispatched from Santa Fé to prevent him from exploring the country north of the Arkansas River, to which the Spanish Government insistently laid claim. However, the expedition failed of its purpose, inasmuch as it marched back up the Arkansas River to the mountains, and returned to Santa Fé without having seen or heard of Lieutenant Pike.

When Colonel Long on his exploring expedition visited this tribe in 1819, he found the Pawnees mourning the loss of a large number of their warriors who had been killed in an encounter with the Cheyennes and Arapahoes in the region adjacent to the Rocky Mountains. It seems that ninety-three warriors left their camp on the Republican River and proceeded on foot to the mountains on a horse-stealing expedition. The party finally reached a point on the south side of the Arkansas River, having up to that time accomplished nothing. Here they were discovered and attacked by a large band of Cheyennes and Arapahoes. During the fight that followed, over fifty of the Pawnees were killed; but the attacking party suffered so severely that after the fighting had continued for a day or more, they were glad to allow the surviving Pawnees, numbering about forty, to escape. Most of the latter were wounded and it was with difficulty that they succeeded in reaching their homes.

All the tribes that I have mentioned were purely nomadic, and, aside from the Pawnees, depended entirely upon game for a living.

The Pawnees were the only tribe that engaged in agriculture. Their summer camps were generally located at some favorable spot for growing corn, beans, pumpkins, and other vegetables. They usually remained at such place until their crops were harvested, when they made large excavations in the ground in which they stored their grain and vegetables for future use. After covering the excavation they carefully obliterated all evidence of it, in order to prevent discovery. They would then go off on hunting expeditions, returning later in the winter to enjoy the fruits of the summer's toil of their squaws—for the warrior never degraded himself by doing any labor which the squaw could perform. Their habitations, when staying any length of time in one locality, were made of poles, brush, grass, and earth, and were more durable structures than the lodges used by the other tribes of the plains.

The Utes, Comanches, Kiowas, Sioux, Cheyennes, and Arapahoes used the conical wigwam, which was easily erected and quickly taken down. The conical wigwam consisted of a framework of small pine poles about two and one-half inches in diameter and twenty feet in length. In its erection, three poles were tied together about two or three feet from the smaller end; the three poles were then set up, their bases forming a triangle sufficiently far apart to permit of a lodge about twenty feet in diameter. The remaining sixteen to eighteen poles used were then placed in position to form a circle, their bases about four feet apart and their tops resting in the fork of the three original poles. Among the plains Indians, where buffalo were plentiful, the covering for this framework consisted of buffalo skins which had been tanned and sewed together by the squaws. It was so shaped that a flap could be thrown back at the top, leaving an opening through which the smoke could escape, and another at the bottom for use as a door. The bottom of this covering was secured by fastening it to small stakes driven into the ground. All of the bedding, buffalo robes, and other belongings of the Indians were taken into the wigwam and piled around the sides; a small hole was then dug in the center of the earthern floor, in which the fire was built. In taking down the tents, preparatory to moving about the country, the squaws removed the covering from the framework, and folded it into a compact bundle; they took the poles down and laid them in two parallel piles three or four feet apart, and then led a pony in between them. The upper end of each pile was fastened to the pack-saddle, leaving the other end to drag upon the ground. Just back of the pony's tail the covering of the tent was fastened to the two sets of poles, on top of which the babies and small children were placed. In this way the Indians moved their camps from place to place. The squaws did all the work of making these tent coverings, procuring the poles, setting up the tents, and taking them down. The warrior never lifted his hand to help, as it was beneath the dignity of a warrior to do any kind of manual labor.

Among the favorite camping-places of the Indians in El Paso County, Colorado, the region extending along the west side of Cheyenne Creek just above its mouth was probably used most frequently. There were evidences of other camping places at different points farther up the creek, that had been used to a lesser extent. Their tent-poles, in being dragged over the country, rapidly wore out, and for that reason the Indians of the plains found it necessary to come to the mountains every year or two to get a new supply. The thousands of small stumps that were to be seen on the side of Cheyenne Mountain at the time of the first settlement of this region gave evidence that many Indians had secured new lodge poles in that locality. It is probable that this was the reason why their tents were so often pitched in the valley of Cheyenne Creek, and undoubtedly this is the origin of the name by which the creek is now known.

On account of its close proximity to the country of the Utes, the Indians of the plains must necessarily have had to come to this locality in very considerable force and must at all times have kept a very sharp lookout in order to avoid disaster. It is known that the Utes maintained pickets in this vicinity much of the time. In the early days, any one climbing to the top of the high sandstone ridge back of the United States Reduction Works at Colorado City might have seen numerous circular places of defense built of loose stone, to a height of four or five feet, and large enough to hold three or four men comfortably. These miniature fortifications were placed at intervals along the ridge all the way from the Fountain to Bear Creek and doubtless were built and used by the Utes. From these small forts, the Indian pickets could overlook the valley of the Fountain, the Mesa, and keep watch over the country for a long distance out on the plains. At such times as the Utes maintained sentinels there it would have been difficult for their enemies to reach this region without being discovered.

CHAPTER II

TRAILS, MINERAL SPRINGS, GAME, ETC.

THE principal Indian trail into the mountains from the plains to the northeast of Pike's Peak came in by way of the Garden Ranch, through what used to be known as Templeton's Gap. It crossed Monument Creek about a mile above Colorado Springs, then followed up a ridge to the Mesa; then it went southwest over the Mesa and across Camp Creek, passing just south of the Garden of the Gods; from there it came down to the Fountain, about a mile west of Colorado City, and there joined another trail that came from the southeast up the east side of Fountain Creek. The latter trail followed the east side of the Fountain from the Arkansas River, and crossed Monument Creek just below the present Artificial Ice Plant in Colorado Springs, from which point it ran along the north side of the Fountain to a point just west of Colorado City, where it crossed to the south side, then up the south side of the creek to the Manitou Springs. From this place it went up Ruxton Creek for a few hundred yards, then crossed over to the west side, then up the creek to a point just below the Colorado Midland Railway bridge; thence westward up a long ravine to its head; then in the same direction near the heads of the ravines running into the Fountain and from a quarter to a half of a mile south of that creek for two miles or more. The trail finally came down to the Fountain again just below Cascade Cañon and from there led up the Fountain to its head, where it branched off in various directions.

The trail I have described from Manitou to Cascade Cañon is the famous old Ute Pass trail which undoubtedly had been used by various tribes of Indians for hundreds of years before the discovery of America. We know it was used later for many generations by the Spanish explorer, the hunter, the trapper, and the Indian until the white settler came, and even after that by occasional war-parties, up to the time the Indians were driven from the State of Colorado. Marble markers were placed at intervals along this trail by the El Paso County Pioneer Society in the summer of 1912. This trail and those leading into it from the plains were well-traveled roads and gave indication of long and frequent use.

Trails, Mineral Springs, Game 29

Dr. Edwin James, botanist and historian of Long's expedition, who visited the Pike's Peak region in 1820, says:

A large and much frequented road passes the springs and enters the mountains running to the north of the high peak.

He says of the principal spring at Manitou:

The boiling spring is a large and beautiful fountain of water, cool and transparent and aërated with carbonic acid. It rises on the brink of a small stream which here descends from the mountains at the point where the bed of this stream divides the ridge of sandstone, which rests against the base of the first granitic range. The water of the spring deposits a copious concretion of carbonate of lime, which has accumulated on every side, until it has formed a large basin overhanging the stream, above which it rises several feet. The basin is of snowy whiteness and large enough to contain three or four hundred gallons, and is constantly overflowing. The spring rises from the bottom of the basin with a rumbling noise, discharging about equal volumes of air and of water, probably about fifty gallons per minute, the whole kept in constant agitation. The water is beautifully transparent, has a sparkling appearance, the grateful taste and exhilarating effect of the most highly aërated artificial mineral water.

In the bottom of the spring a great number of beads and other small articles of Indian adornment were found, having unquestionably been left there as a sacrifice or present to the springs, which are regarded with a sort of veneration by the savages. Bijeau, our guide, assured us he had repeatedly taken beads and other adornments from these springs and sold them to the same savages who had thrown them in.

Mr. Rufus B. Sage, who describes himself as a New Englander, after passing through this region in 1842, published a book giving his experiences and observations. In speaking of the Fontaine qui Bouille Creek, now known as the Fountain and of the Manitou Springs, he says:

This name is derived from two singular springs situated within a few yards of each other at the creek's head, both of which emit water in the form of vapor, with a hissing noise; one strongly impregnated with sulphur and the other with soda. The soda water is fully as good as any manufactured for special use and sparkles and foams with equal effervescence. The Arapahoes regard this phenomenon with awe, and venerate it as the manifestation of the immediate presence of the Great Spirit. They call it the "Medicine Fountain" and seldom neglect to bestow their gifts upon it whenever an opportunity is presented. These offerings usually consist of robes, blankets, arrows, bows, knives, beads, moccasins, etc., which they either throw into the water, or hang upon the surrounding trees.

Sometimes a whole village will visit the place for the purpose of paying their united regard to this sacred fountain.

The scenery in the vicinity is truly magnificent. A valley several hundred yards in width heads at the springs, and overlooking it from the west in almost perpendicular ascent tower the lofty summits of Pike's Peak, piercing the clouds and reveling in eternal snow. This valley opens eastward and is walled in at the right and left at the mountain's base by a stretch of high table-land surmounted by oaks and stately pines, with now and then an interval displaying a luxuriant coating of grass. The soil is a reddish loam and very rich. The trees, which skirt the creek as it traces its way from the fountain, are generally free from underbrush, and show almost as much regularity of position as if planted by the hand of art. A lusty growth of vegetation is sustained among them to their very trunks, which is garnished by wild flowers during the summer months, that invest the whole scene with an enchantment peculiar to itself.

The climate, too, is far milder in this than in adjoining regions, even of a more southern latitude. "'T is here summer first unfolds her robes, and here the longest tarries"; the grass, continuing green the entire winter, here first feels the genial touch of spring. Snow seldom remains upon the ground to exceed a single day, even in the severest weather, while the neighboring hills and prairies present their white mantlings for weeks in succession.

As the creek emerges from the mountains, it increases in size by the accession of several tributaries, and the valley also expands, retaining for a considerable distance the distinguishing traces above described.

The vicinity affords an abundance of game, among which are deer, sheep, bear, antelope, elk, and buffalo, together with turkeys, geese, ducks, grouse, mountain fowls, and rabbits. Affording as it does such magnificent and delightful scenery, such rich stores for the supply of human wants both to please the taste and enrapture the heart; so heavenlike in its appearance and character, it is no wonder the untaught savage reveres it as a place wherein the Good Spirit delights to dwell, and hastens with his free-will offerings to the strange fountain, in the full belief that its bubbling waters are the more immediate impersonation of Him whom he adores.

And there are other scenes adjoining this that demand a passing notice. A few miles from the springs, and running parallel with the eastern base of the mountain range, several hundred yards removed from it, a wall of coarse, red granite towers to a varied height of from fifty to three hundred feet. This wall is formed of an immense strata planted vertically. This mural tier is isolated and occupies its prairie site in silent majesty, as if to guard the approach to the stupendous monuments of Nature's handiwork, that form the background, disclosing itself to the beholder for a distance of over thirty miles.

Lieut. John C. Frémont, who visited the springs in 1843, while on his second expedition, was just as enthusiastic about them. He says:

On the morning of the 16th of July we resumed our journey. Our direction was up the Boiling Springs River, it being my intention to visit the celebrated springs from which the river takes its name, and which are on its upper waters at the foot of Pike's Peak.

Our animals fared well while we were on this stream,

there being everywhere a great abundance of grass. Beautiful clusters of flowering plants were numerous, and wild currants, nearly ripe, were abundant. On the afternoon of the 17th, we entered among the broken ridges at the foot of the mountain, where the river made several forks.

Leaving the camp to follow slowly, I rode ahead in the afternoon, in search of the springs. In the meantime, the clouds, which had been gathering all the afternoon over the mountains, began to roll down their sides, and a storm so violent burst upon me that it appeared I had entered the store house of the thunder storms. I continued, however, to ride along up the river until about sunset, and was beginning to be doubtful of finding the springs before the next day, when I came suddenly upon a large, smooth rock about twenty feet in diameter, where the water from several springs was bubbling and boiling up in the midst of a white encrustation, with which it had covered a portion of the rock. As it did not correspond with the description given me by the hunters, I did not stop to taste the water, but dismounting, walked a little way up the river, and passing through a narrow thicket of shrubbery bordering the stream, stepped directly upon a huge, white rock at the foot of which the river, already becoming a torrent, foamed along, broken by a small fall.

A deer which had been drinking at the spring was startled by my approach, and springing across the river bounded off up the mountain. In the upper part of the rock, which had been formed by the deposition, was a beautiful, white basin overhung by currant bushes, in which the cold, clear water bubbled up, kept in constant motion by the escaping gas, and overflowing the rock which it had almost entirely covered with a smooth crust of glistening white.

I had all day refrained from drinking, reserving myself for the springs, and as I could not well be more wet than the rain had already made me, I lay down by the side of the basin and drank heartily of the delightful water.

As it was now beginning to grow dark, I rode quickly down the river on which I found the camp a few miles below. The morning of the 18th was beautiful and clear, and all of the people being anxious to drink of these famous waters, we encamped immediately at the springs and spent there a very pleasant day.

On the opposite side of the river is another locality of springs which are entirely of the same nature. The water has a very agreeable taste, which Mr. Preuss found very much to resemble that of the famous Selter spring in the Grand Duchy of Nassau, a country famous for wine and mineral waters.

Resuming our journey on the morning of the 19th, we descended the river, in order to reach the mouth of the eastern fork which I proposed to ascend. The left bank of the river is here very much broken. There is a handsome little bottom on the right, and both banks are exceedingly picturesque, a stratum of red rock in nearly perpendicular walls, crossing the valley from north to south.

Lieut. George F. Ruxton, an officer of the British Army, who was seeking the restoration of his health by roughing it in the Rocky Mountains, camped at the Manitou Springs for a number of months in the early part of 1847.

Trails, Mineral Springs, Game

Writing of his trip from Pueblo up the Fontaine qui Bouille in the month of March of that year, and of his stay at the springs afterwards, he says:

The further I advanced up the creek and the nearer the mountains, the more advanced was the vegetation. As yet, however, the cottonwoods and the larger trees in the bottom showed no signs of life, and the currant and cherry bushes still looked dry and sapless. The thickets, however, were filled with birds and resounded with their songs, and the plains were alive with prairie dogs, busy in repairing their houses and barking lustily as I rode through their towns. Turkeys, too, were calling in the timber, and the boom of the prairie fowl at rise and set of sun was heard on every side. The snow had entirely disappeared from the plains, but Pike's Peak and the mountains were still clad in white.

On my way I met a band of hunters who had been driven in by a party of Arapahoes who were encamped on the eastern fork of the Fontaine qui Bouille [Monument Creek]. They strongly urged me to return, as, being alone, I could not fail to be robbed of my animals, if not killed myself. However, in pursuance of my fixed rule never to stop on account of Indians, I proceeded up the river and camped on the first fork for a day or two, hunting in the mountains. I then moved up the main fork on which I had been directed by the hunters to proceed, in order to visit the far famed springs, from which the creek takes its name. I followed a very good lodge-pole trail which struck the creek before entering the broken country, being that used by the Utes and Arapahoes on their way to the

Bayou Salado. Here the valley narrowed considerably, and turning an angle with the creek, I was at once shut in by mountains and elevated ridges which rose on each side of the stream. This was now a rapid torrent tumbling over the rocks and stones and fringed with oak and a shrubbery of brush. A few miles on, the cañon opened into a little shelving glade and on the right bank of the stream, raised several feet above it, was a flat, white rock, in which was a round hole where one of the celebrated springs hissed and bubbled with its escaping gas. I had been cautioned against drinking this, being directed to follow the stream a few yards to another, which is the true soda spring.

I had not only abstained from drinking that day, but with the aid of a handful of salt, which I had brought with me for the purpose, had so highly seasoned my breakfast of venison, that I was in a most satisfactory state of thirst. I therefore proceeded at once to the other spring, and found it about forty yards from the first and immediately above the river, issuing from a little basin in the flat, white rock, and trickling over the edge into the stream. The escape of gas in this was much stronger than in the other, and was similar to water boiling smartly.

I had provided myself with a tin cup holding about a pint, but before dipping it in I divested myself of my pouch and belt, and sat down in order to enjoy the draught at my leisure. I was half dead with thirst, and tucking up the sleeves of my hunting shirt, I dipped the cup into the midst of the bubbles and raised it, hissing and sparkling, to my lips. Such a draught! Three times without drawing a breath was it replenished and emptied, almost blowing up the roof of my mouth with its effervescence. It was equal to the very best soda water, but possesses that fresh, natural flavor which manufactured water cannot impart.

The Indians regard with awe the medicine waters of these fountains, as being the abode of a Spirit who breathes through the transparent water, and thus by his exhalations causes the perturbation of its surface. The Arapahoes especially attribute to this water god, the power of ordaining the success or miscarriage of their war expeditions, and as their braves pass often by the mysterious springs when in search of their hereditary enemies, the Utes, in the "Valley of Salt," they never fail to bestow their votive offerings upon the water sprite, in order to propitiate the Manitou of the fountain and insure a fortunate issue to their path of war. Thus at the time of my visit, the basin of the spring was filled with beads and wampum and pieces of red cloth and knives, while the surrounding trees were hung with strips of deer skin, cloth, and moccasins; to which, had they been serviceable, I would most sacrilegiously have helped myself. The signs, too, around the spring, plainly showed that here a war dance had been executed by the braves, and I was not a little pleased to find that they had already been here and were not likely to return the same way; but in this supposition I was quite astray.

The large spring referred to by Dr. James, Sage, Frémont, Ruxton, and the other writers whom I have quoted, is the one now enclosed and used by the bottling works at Manitou. Ruxton says the two springs were intimately connected with the separation of the Comanche and the Snake, or

Ute tribes, and he gives the following legend concerning the beginning of the trouble:

Many hundreds of winters ago, when the cottonwoods on the Big River were no higher than an arrow, and the red men, who hunted the buffalo on the plains, all spoke the same language, and the pipe of peace breathed its social cloud of kinnikinnik whenever two parties of hunters met on the boundless plains—when, with hunting grounds and game of every kind in the greatest abundance, no nation dug up the hatchet with another because one of its hunters followed the game into their bounds, but, on the contrary, loaded for him his back with choice and fattest meat, and ever proffered the soothing pipe before the stranger, with well-filled belly, left the village,—it happened that two hunters of different nations met one day on a small rivulet, where both had repaired to quench their thirst. A little stream of water, rising from a spring on a rock within a few feet of the bank, trickled over it and fell splashing into the river. To this the hunters repaired; and while one sought the spring itself, where the water, cold and clear, reflected on its surface the image of the surrounding scenery, the other, tired by his exertions in the chase, threw himself at once to the ground and plunged his face into the running stream.

The latter had been unsuccessful in the chase, and perhaps his bad fortune and the sight of the fat deer, which the other hunter threw from his back before he drank at the crystal spring, caused a feeling of jealousy and ill-humour to take possession of his mind. The other, on the contrary, before he satisfied his thirst,

Trails, Mineral Springs, Game 39

raised in the hollow of his hand a portion of the water, and, lifting it towards the sun, reversed his hand and allowed it to fall upon the ground,—a libation to the Great Spirit who had vouchsafed him a successful hunt, and the blessing of the refreshing water with which he was about to quench his thirst.

Seeing this, and being reminded that he had neglected the usual offering, only increased the feeling of envy and annoyance which the unsuccessful hunter permitted to get the mastery of his heart; and the Evil Spirit at that moment entering his body, his temper fairly flew away, and he sought some pretense by which to provoke a quarrel with the stranger Indian at the spring.

"Why does a stranger," he asked, rising from the stream at the same time, "drink at the spring-head, when one to whom the fountain belongs contents himself with the water that runs from it?"

"The Great Spirit places the cool water at the spring," answered the other hunter, "that his children may drink it pure and undefiled. The running water is for the beasts which scour the plains. Au-sa-qua is a chief of the Shos-shone; he drinks at the head water."

"The Shos-shone is but a tribe of the Comanche," returned the other; "Waco-mish leads the grand nation. Why does a Shos-shone dare to drink above him?"

"He has said it. The Shos-shone drinks at the spring-head; other nations of the stream which runs into the fields. Au-sa-qua is chief of his nation. The Comanche are brothers. Let them both drink of the same water."

"The Shos-shone pays tribute to the Comanche.

Waco-mish leads that nation to war. Waco-mish is chief of the Shos-shone, as he is of his own people."

"Waco-mish lies; his tongue is forked like the rattlesnake's; his heart is black as the Misho-tunga [bad spirit]. When the Manitou made his children, whether Shos-shone or Comanche, Arapahoe, Shi-an, or Pā-né, he gave them buffalo to eat, and the pure water of the fountain to quench their thirst. He said not to one, Drink here, and to another, Drink there; but gave the crystal spring to all, that all might drink."

Waco-mish almost burst with rage as the other spoke; but his coward heart alone prevented him from provoking an encounter with the calm Shos-shone. *He*, made thirsty by the words he had spoken—for the red man is ever sparing of his tongue—again stooped down to the spring to quench his thirst, when the subtle warrior of the Comanche suddenly threw himself upon the kneeling hunter, and, forcing his head into the bubbling water, held him down with all his strength, until his victim no longer struggled, his stiffened limbs relaxed, and he fell forward over the spring, drowned and dead.

Over the body stood the murderer, and no sooner was the deed of blood consummated than bitter remorse took possession of his mind, where before had reigned the fiercest passion and vindictive hate. With hands clasped to his forehead, he stood transfixed with horror, intently gazing on his victim, whose head still remained immersed in the fountain. Mechanically he dragged the body a few paces from the water, which, as soon as the head of the dead Indian was withdrawn, the Comanche saw suddenly and strangely disturbed. Bubbles sprang up from the bottom, and rising to the surface, escaped in hissing gas. A thin vapoury cloud arose, and gradually dissolving, displayed to the eyes of the trembling murderer the figure of an aged Indian, whose long, snowy hair and venerable beard, blown aside by a gentle air from his breast, discovered the well-known totem of the great Wan-kan-aga, the father of the Comanche and Shos-shone nation, whom the tradition of the tribe, handed down by skillful hieroglyphics, almost deified for the good actions and deeds of bravery this famous warrior had performed when on earth.

Stretching out a war-club towards the affrighted murderer, the figure thus addressed him:

"Accursed of my tribe! this day thou hast severed the link between the mightiest nations of the world, while the blood of the brave Shos-shone cries to the Manitou for vengeance. May the water of thy tribe be rank and bitter in their throats." Thus saying, and swinging his ponderous war-club (made from the elk's horn) round his head, he dashed out the brains of the Comanche, who fell headlong into the spring, which, from that day to the present moment, remains rank and nauseous, so that not even when half dead with thirst, can one drink the foul water of that spring.

The good Wan-kan-aga, however, to perpetuate the memory of the Shos-shone warrior, who was renowned in his tribe for valour and nobleness of heart, struck, with the same avenging club, a hard, flat rock which overhung the rivulet, just out of sight of this scene of blood; and forthwith the rock opened into a round, clear basin, which instantly filled with bubbling, sparkling water, than which no thirsty hunter ever drank a sweeter or a cooler draught.

Thus the two springs remain, an everlasting memento of the foul murder of the brave Shos-shone, and the stern justice of the good Wan-kan-aga; and from that day the two mighty tribes of the Shos-shone and Comanche have remained severed and apart; although a long and bloody war followed the treacherous murder of the Shos-shone chief, and many a scalp torn from the head of the Comanche paid the penalty of his death.

In telling of the great quantities of game in this region, Ruxton says:

Never was there such a paradise for hunters as this lone and solitary spot.

Game abounded on every hand. Bear, elk, deer, mountain sheep, antelope, and grouse were in abundance in the surrounding mountains and valleys. Of buffalo there were few except in the valleys west of Pike's Peak and in the Bayou Salado, or South Park, as it is now known.

Ruxton further says:

It is a singular fact that within the last two years the prairies, extending from the mountains to one hundred miles or more down the Arkansas, have been entirely abandoned by the buffalo; indeed, in crossing from the settlements of New Mexico, the boundary of their former range is marked by skulls and bones, which appear fresher as the traveler advances westward and towards the waters of the Platte.

The evidences that Ruxton here mentions were

still apparent twelve or fourteen years later, when the first settlers of this region arrived. Buffalo skulls and bones were scattered everywhere over the plains, but live buffalo could seldom be found nearer than one hundred miles east of the mountains.

The reason for this has been variously stated, some claiming that a contagious disease broke out among the buffalo in the early forties, which virtually exterminated those along the eastern base of the mountains. Others say that about that time there was a tremendous snowfall in the early part of the winter which covered the whole country along the eastern base of the mountains to a depth of six to eight feet, and that as a result all the buffalo within the region of the snowfall starved to death during the following winter. It is very possible that the latter reason may have been the true one, as a heavy fall of snow in the early part of the winter is not unknown. In the winter of 1864–1865 the antelope of this region nearly starved to death, owing to a two-foot fall of snow, on the last day of October and the first day of November, 1864, which covered the ground to a considerable depth for most of the winter.

While it is true that there were no buffalo in

this immediate region at the time Ruxton was here, nor afterwards, it is well-known that they had been fairly plentiful in earlier years. Lieutenant Pike tells of killing five buffalo the day he reached the present site of Pueblo in 1806, and a day or two afterwards he killed three more on Turkey Creek, about twenty miles south of where Colorado Springs now stands, and saw others while climbing the mountains in his attempt to reach the "high point," as he calls it, now known as Pike's Peak.

In 1820, Long's expedition, on its way from Platte Cañon, killed several buffalo on Monument Creek, a few miles south of the Divide; and later, while camped on the Fountain a short distance below the site of the present city of Colorado Springs, killed several more.

Sage says that in 1842, during a five days' stay at Jimmy's Camp (ten miles east of the present city of Colorado Springs), he "killed three fine buffalo cows."

After Ruxton had been camped near Manitou Springs for two or three weeks, while out hunting one day, he ran across an Indian camp, which startled him very much. No Indians were in sight at the time, but later he got a glimpse of two carrying in a deer which they had killed. The

Trails, Mineral Springs, Game 45

next morning Ruxton concluded that as a matter of safety, he had better remove his camp to some more secluded spot. The following day a fire was started on the side of the mountain to the south of the springs, which rapidly spread in every direction. He says:

I had from the first no doubt that the fire was caused by the Indians who had probably discovered my animals, and thinking that a large party of hunters might be out, had taken advantage of a favorable wind to set fire to the grass, hoping to secure the horses and mules in the confusion, without risk of attacking the camp.

In order to be out of reach of the fire, Ruxton moved his camp down the Fontaine qui Bouille six or seven miles. He says:

All this time the fire was spreading out on the prairies. It extended at least five miles on the left bank of the creek and on the right was more slowly creeping up the mountainside, while the brush and timber in the bottom was one mass of flame. Besides the long, sweeping line of the advancing flame the plateaus on the mountainside and within the line were burning in every direction as the squalls and eddies down the gullies drove the fire to all points. The mountains themselves being invisible, the air from the low ground where I then was, appeared a mass of fire, and huge crescents of flame danced as it were in the very sky, until a mass of timber blazing at once exhibited the somber background of the stupendous mountains.

The fire extended towards the waters of the Platte upwards of forty miles, and for fourteen days its glare was visible on the Arkansas River fifty miles distant.

The testimony of Ruxton bears out information I have from other sources, that a large portion of the great areas of dead timber on the mountainsides of this region is the result of fires started by the various Indian tribes in their wanderings to and fro. Old trappers say that the Utes frequently went out upon the plains on horse-stealing expeditions; that when they had located a camp of their enemies, they would stealthily creep in among their ponies in the night, round them up, and start off towards the mountains with as many as they could hastily gather together. They were sure to be pursued the following morning when the raid had been discovered, and often the Utes with the stolen herd would find their pursuers close after them by the time they reached the mountains. In that case, they knew that if they followed up Ute Pass they were likely to be overtaken, but by crossing over the northern point of Cheyenne Mountain and on to the west along a trail that ran not very far distant from the route now followed by the Cripple Creek Short Line, they could much more easily elude their pursuers. If, when west of Cheyenne Mountain the Utes found their enemies gaining upon them, they would start a timber fire to cover their retreat. These fires would, of course, spread indefinitely and ruin immense tracts of timber. This is doubtless one of the principal reasons why our mountainsides are so nearly denuded of their original growth of trees. These horse-stealing raids were no uncommon occurrence. Colonel Dodge, in his book *Our Wild Indians*, tells of one made by the Utes in 1874, which was daring as well as successful. He says:

A mixed band of some fifteen hundred Sioux and Cheyennes, hunting in 1874, went well up on the headwaters of the Republican River in search of buffalo. The Utes found them out and a few warriors slipped into their camp during the night, stampeded their ponies at daylight, and in spite of the hot pursuit of the Sioux, reached the mountains with over two hundred head.

Ruxton frequently mentions the Ute Pass, and states that it was the principal line of travel to and from the South Park for all the Indian tribes of this region at the time of his arrival, as well as previous thereto.

There was another much-used trail into the South Park which entered the mountains near the present town of Cañon City. It led in a northwesterly direction from the latter place, and reached the South Park proper near Hartsell Hot Springs. This route was used by the Indians occupying the country along the Arkansas River and to the south of it. In addition to the two principal trails, there were others of lesser note, as, for example, that over the north end of Cheyenne Mountain, and one west of the present town of Monument; but these were difficult and were not used to any great extent.

In 1806, Lieutenant Pike attempted to lead his exploring expedition over the Cañon City trail, but evidently had a very poor guide, and, as a result, lost his way very soon after leaving the Arkansas River. They wandered about through the low mountains west of the present mining camp of Cripple Creek, and finally reached the Platte near the west end of Eleven-Mile Cañon where the river emerges from the South Park. He mentions having found near that point a recently abandoned Indian camp which he estimates must have been occupied by at least three thousand Indians.

Thomas J. Farnham, on his way to Oregon in

Trails, Mineral Springs, Game 49

1839, passed through the South Park, reaching it from the Arkansas River by the trail already described. He tells of his trip, in a rudely bound little book of minutely fine print, published in 1843. In recounting his journey from the Arkansas River to the South Park, he frequently mentions James Peak as being to the east of the route he was traveling. Previously, when encamped on the Arkansas River, below the mouth of the Fontaine qui Bouille, he speaks of the latter stream as heading in James Peak, eighty miles to the northwest; he also states that one of the branches of the Huerfano originates in Pike's Peak, seventy to eighty miles to the south. This brings to mind the fact that previous to about 1840 the peak that we now know as Pike's Peak was known as James Peak. Major S. H. Long, who was in command of the expedition that explored the Pike's Peak region in 1820, gave it this name in honor of Dr. James, who is supposed to have been the first white man to ascend it. After about 1840, this name was gradually dropped and Pike's Peak was substituted.

Farnham was very much pleased with the South Park, and says of it, after describing its streams, valleys, and rocky ridges:

This is a bird's-eye view of Bayou Salado, so named

from the circumstance that native rock salt is found in some parts of it. We were in the central portion of it. To the north and south and west its isolated plains rise one above another, always beautiful and covered with verdure during the months of spring and summer. A sweet spot this, for the romance of the future as well as of the present and past. The buffalo have for ages resorted here about the last days of July from the arid plains of the Arkansas and the Platte; and hither the Utes, Cheyennes and Arapahoes, Black Feet, Crows and Sioux of the north, have for ages met and hunted and fought and loved, and when their battles and hunts were interrupted by the chills and snows of November, they separated for their several winter resorts.

How wild and beautiful the past, as it comes up fledged with the rich plumage of the imagination! These vales, studded with a thousand villages of conical skin wigwams, with their thousands of fires blazing on the starry brow of night! I see the dusky forms crouching around the glowing piles of ignited logs, in family groups, whispering the dreams of their rude love, or gathered around the stalwart form of some noble chief at the hour of midnight, listening to the harangue of vengeance or the whoop of war that is to cast the deadly arrow with the first gleam of morning light.

Or, may we not see them gathered, a circle of old braves, around an aged tree, surrounded each by the musty trophies of half a century's daring deeds. The eldest and richest in scalps rises from the center of the ring and advances to the tree. Hear him!

"Fifty winters ago when the seventh moon's first horn hung over the green forests of the Ute hills, myself and five others erected a lodge for the Great Spirit on the snows of the White Butte and carried there our wampum and skins, and the hide of a white buffalo. We hung them in the Great Spirit's lodge and seated ourselves in silence till the moon had descended the western mountain, and thought of the blood of our fathers that the Comanches had killed when the moon was round and lay on the eastern plains. My own father was scalped, and the fathers of five others were scalped, and their bloody heads were gnawed by the wolf. We could not live while our father's lodges were empty and the scalps of their murderers were not in the lodges of our mothers. Our hearts told us to make these offerings to the Great Spirit who had fostered them on the mountains, and when the moon was down and the shadows of the White Butte were as dark as the hair of a bear, we said to the Great Spirit: 'No man can war with the arrows from the quiver of thy storms. No man's word can be heard when thy voice is among the clouds. No man's hand is strong when thy hand lets loose the wind. The wolf gnaws the heads of our fathers and the scalps of their murderers hang not in the lodges of our mothers. Great Father Spirit, send not thine anger out. Hold in thy hand the winds. Let not thy great voice drown the death yell while we hunt the murderers of our fathers.' I and the five others then built in the middle of the lodge a fire, and in its bright light the Great Spirit saw the wampum and the skins and the white buffalo hide. Five days and nights I and five others danced and smoked the medicine and beat the board with sticks and chanted away the powers of the great Medicine Men, that they might not be evil to us and bring sickness into our bones. Then when the stars were shining in the clear sky, we swore (I must not tell what, for it was in the ear of the Great Spirit), and went out of the lodge with our bosoms full of anger against the murderers of our fathers whose bones were in the jaws of the wolf and went for their scalps, to hang them in the lodges of our mothers." See him strike the aged tree with his war-club; again, again, nine times. "So many Comanches did I slay, the murderers of my father, before the moon was round again and lay upon the eastern plains."

Farnham, continuing, says:

This is not merely an imaginary scene of former times in the Bayou Salado. All the essential incidents related happened yearly in that and other hunting-grounds, whenever the old braves assembled to celebrate valorous deeds of their younger days. When these exciting relations were finished, the young men of the tribe who had not yet distinguished themselves were exhorted to seek glory in a similar way; and woe to him who passed his manhood without ornamenting the door of his lodge with the scalps of his enemies.

This valley is still frequented by these Indians as a summer haunt, when the heat of the plains renders them uncomfortable. The Utes were scouring it when we passed. Our guide informed us that the Utes reside on both sides of the mountains,—that they are continually migrating from one side to the other,—that they speak the Spanish language,—that some few half-breeds have embraced the Catholic faith,—that the remainder yet hold the simple and sublime faith of their forefathers, in the existence of one great, creating, and sustaining Cause, mingled

Trails, Mineral Springs, Game

with the belief in the ghostly visitations of their deceased Medicine Men, or Diviners;—that they number one thousand families.

He also stated that the Cheyennes were less brave and more thievish than any of the other tribes living on the plains.

Farnham's description of the incantations practiced by the Utes is in the main probably true; the information on which it was based was doubtless obtained from his guide.

Ruxton tells of the use of the trail west of the present town of Monument by a war-party of Arapahoes on their way to the South Park to fight the Utes. In the night the band had surprised a small company of trappers on the head of Bijou Creek, killing four of them and capturing all of their horses. The following morning two of the trappers, one of whom was slightly wounded, started in pursuit of the Indians, intending if possible to recover their animals. They followed the trail of the Indians to a point in the neighborhood of the present town of Monument where they found that the band had divided, the larger party, judging from the direction taken, evidently intending to enter the mountains by way of Ute Pass. The other party, having all the loose animals, started across the mountains by the pass to the west of Monument, probably hoping to get the better of the Utes by coming in from two different directions. The trappers followed the latter party across the first mountains where they found their stolen animals in charge of three Indians. The trappers surprised and killed all three of them, recaptured their animals, and then hurried on to the Utes, giving such timely warning as enabled them to defeat the Arapahoes in a very decisive manner.

The battles in the South Park and on the plains between the contending tribes were seldom of a very sanguinary nature. If the attacking Indians happened to find their enemies on level ground, they would circle around them just out of gunshot at first, gradually coming closer, all the time lying on the outside and shooting from under the necks of their ponies. These ponies were generally the best that the tribe afforded and were not often used except for purposes of war. While engaged in battle, the Indians seldom used saddles, and in place of bridles had merely a piece of plaited buffalo-hide rope, tied around the under jaw of the pony. If the defending party was located in a fairly good defensive position, the battle consisted of groups of the attacking party dashing in, firing, and then dashing out again.

Trails, Mineral Springs, Game 55

This was kept up until a few warriors had been killed or wounded and a few scalps had been taken; then the battle was over, one side or the other retreating. With an Indian, it was a waste of time to kill an enemy unless his scalp was taken, as that was the evidence necessary to prove the prowess of the warrior. Engagements of the kind I have mentioned have occurred in almost every valley in and around the South Park at some time during the hundreds of years of warfare that was carried on in that region.

Frémont, on his return trip from California, during his second exploring expedition, crossed the Rocky Mountains by way of Middle Park, then across South Park, reaching the Arkansas River near the present town of Cañon City. On his way through the South Park he witnessed one of these battles, in describing which he says:

In the evening a band of buffalo furnished a little excitement by charging through our camp. On the following day we descended the stream by an excellent buffalo trail along the open grassy bottom of the river. On our right, the Bayou was bordered by a mountainous range crested with rocky and naked peaks, and below it had a beautiful parklike character of pretty, level prairies, interspersed among low spurs, wooded openly with pine and quaking asps, contrasting well with the denser pines which swept around on the mountainous sides. Descending always the valley of the stream, towards noon we descried a mounted party descending the point of a spur, and judging them to be Arapahoes—who, defeated or victorious, were equally dangerous to us, and with whom a fight would be inevitable—we hurried to post ourselves as strongly as possible on some willow islands in the river. We had scarcely halted when they arrived, proving to be a party of Ute women, who told us that on the other side of the ridge their village was fighting with the Arapahoes. As soon as they had given us this information, they filled the air with cries and lamentations, which made us understand that some of their chiefs had been killed.

Extending along the river directly ahead of us was a low piny ridge, leaving between it and the stream a small open bottom on which the Utes had very injudiciously placed their village, which, according to the women, numbered about three hundred warriors. Advancing in the cover of the pines, the Arapahoes, about daylight, charged into the village, driving off a great number of their horses, and killing four men, among them the principal chief of the village. They drove the horses perhaps a mile beyond the village to the end of a hollow where they had previously forted at the edge of the pines. Here the Utes had instantly attacked them in turn, and, according to the report of the women, were getting rather the best of the day. The women pressed us eagerly to join with their people, and would immediately have provided us with the best horses at the village, but it was not for us to interfere in such a conflict. Neither party were our friends or under our protection, and each was ready to prey upon us that could. But we could not help feeling an unusual excitement at being within a few hundred yards of a fight in which five hundred men were closely engaged, and hearing the sharp cracks of their rifles. We were in a bad position and subject to be attacked in it. Either party which we might meet, victorious or defeated, was certain to fall upon us, and gearing up immediately, we kept close along the pines of the ridge, having it between us and the village, and keeping the scouts on the summit to give us notice of the approach of the Indians. As we passed by the village which was immediately below us, horsemen were galloping to and fro, and groups of people were gathered around those who were wounded and dead and who were being brought in from the field.

We continued to press on, and crossing another fork which came in from the right, after having made fifteen miles from the village, fortified ourselves strongly in the pines a short distance from the river.

During the afternoon Pike's Peak had been plainly in view before us and from our encampment bore north 87° east by compass. This was a familiar object, and it had for us the face of an old friend. At its foot were the springs where we had spent a pleasant day in coming out.

In 1859, a battle between the Utes on the one side, and the Cheyennes, Arapahoes, and Sioux on the other, was fought six miles north of Colorado City, in the valley now occupied by the Modern Woodmen's Home. There were several hundred warriors on each side and the battle was of unusual duration, continuing for almost an entire day. The Utes were finally victorious and drove their enemies back to the plains.

Until 1864, every spring after the white settlers came into this region, war-parties of Cheyennes, Arapahoes, and Sioux would come trailing in from the plains, pass through Colorado City, stopping long enough to beg food from the families living near the line of their march and then go on to the soda springs; here they would tarry long enough to make an offering to the Great Spirit who was supposed to be manifest in the bubbling waters, and then follow, in single file, up the Ute Pass trail into the South Park, where they would scout around until they had found a band of Utes. If they succeeded in surprising the latter, they would probably come back with a lot of extra ponies and sometimes with captured squaws and children, in which case they would exhibit a jubilant air; but at other times on their return, they would present such a dejected appearance that one could readily surmise that they had suffered defeat. These annual visits were discontinued after the tribes became involved in warfare with the whites.

Referring again to the mineral springs at Manitou, I quote from Col. R. B. Marcy, of the United States Army, who, with his command, camped

Trails, Mineral Springs, Game

there during the whole of the month of April, 1858. He tells not only of the springs and the game of that neighborhood, but of a frightful snowstorm that delayed them, near Eastonville in El Paso County, for several days at the beginning of the following month. He says:

> Having accomplished the objects of my mission to New Mexico, by procuring animals and other supplies sufficient to enable the troops at Fort Bridger to make an early march into Salt Lake Valley, I, on the 15th day of March, left Fort Union on my return for Utah, intending to pass around the eastern base of the mountains near Pike's Peak and the headwaters of the Arkansas and Platte rivers, following the Cherokee trail from the Cache la Poudre. The command was well organized, and we made rapid progress for about two hundred and fifty miles, when, on the 27th of March, I received an order from the General in Command in New Mexico, to halt and await reinforcements. I was obliged to obey the order and went into camp upon the headwaters of a small tributary of the Arkansas, called Fontaine qui Bouille, directly at the foot of Pike's Peak and near a very peculiar spring which gives the name to the stream.
>
> This beautiful fountain issues from the center of a basin, or rather bowl, about six feet in diameter, and throws out a column of water near the size of a man's arm. The receptacle, which is constantly filled but never runs over, seems to have been formed by the deposit of salts from the water, and is as perfectly symmetrical and round as if it had been cut

out with a chisel. As the fountain is constantly playing and never overflows, it of course has a subterranean outlet. The most remarkable feature, however, in the Fontaine qui Bouille, is the peculiar taste of the water. It is pungent and sparkling and somewhat similar in taste to the water from the Congress spring at Saratoga, but sweeter, and to my palate pleasanter. We drank it every day in large quantities without perceiving any ill effect from it, and the men made use of it instead of yeast in raising their bread, which induced the belief that it contained soda or some other alkali.

The Indians believe it to possess some mysterious powers, the purport of which I could not learn, but there were a great many arrows, pieces of cloth, and other articles that they had deposited in the spring, probably as an offering to the Big Medicine Genius that presided over it. We remained at this place a month, during which time we amused ourselves in hunting elk, mountain sheep, and blacktail deer, all of which were very abundant in the surrounding country, and our larder was constantly supplied with the most delicious game.

I remember that one morning just at daybreak, I was awakened by my servant, who told me there was a large herd of elk in close proximity to the camp. I ran out as soon as possible and saw at least five hundred of these magnificent animals, drawn up in line like a troop of cavalry horses, with their heads all turned in the same direction, and from the crest of a high projecting cliff, looking in apparent wonder and bewilderment directly down upon us. It was to me a most novel and interesting spectacle. The noise made in the camp soon frightened them, however,

Ouray
Chief of the Utes

and they started for the mountains. They were pursued for some distance by our hunters, who succeeded in killing six before they escaped.

On the 30th day of April, our reinforcements having joined us, we gladly resumed our march for Utah, and at about one o'clock encamped upon the ridge that divides the Arkansas from the Platte rivers. The day was bright, cheerful, and pleasant, the atmosphere soft, balmy, and delightful. The fresh grass was about six inches high. The trees had put forth their new leaves and all nature conspired in giving evidence that the somber garb of winter had been cast aside for the more verdant and smiling attire of spring. Our large herds of animals were turned out to graze upon the tender and nutritious grass that everywhere abounded. Our men were enjoying their social jokes and pastimes after the fatigues of the day's march and everything indicated contentment and happiness. This pleasant state of things lasted until near sunset, when the wind suddenly changed into the north. It turned cold and soon commenced snowing violently, and continued to increase until it became a frightful winter tempest, filling the atmosphere with a dense cloud of driving snow, against which it was utterly impossible to ride or walk. Soon after the storm set in, one of our herds of three hundred horses and mules broke furiously away from the herdsmen who were guarding them, and in spite of their utmost efforts, ran at full speed directly with the wind for fifty miles before they stopped. Three of the herdsmen followed them as far as they were able, but soon became exhausted, bewildered, and lost on the prairie. One of them succeeded in finding his way back to camp in a state of great prostration and suffering. One of the others was found frozen to death in the snow, and the third was discovered crawling about upon his hands and knees in a state of temporary delirium, after the tempest subsided. This terrific storm exceeded in violence and duration anything of the kind our eldest mountaineer had ever beheld. It continued with uninterrupted fury for sixty consecutive hours and during this time it was impossible to move for any distance facing the wind and snow. One of our employes who went out about two hundred yards from the camp, set out to return, but was unable to do so and perished in the attempt. Several antelope were found frozen upon the prairie after the storm. . . . At the termination of this frightful tempest, there was about three feet of snow upon the ground, but the warm rays of the sun soon melted it, and after collecting together our stampeded animals, we again set forward for Utah and on the third day following, struck the South Platte at its confluence with Cherry Creek. There was at that time but one white man living within one hundred and fifty miles of the place, and he was an Indian trader named Jack Audeby, on the Arkansas.

A year later, after the Pike's Peak mining excitement had started, Marcy issued a handbook for overland expeditions, in which he says, referring to a point at the mouth of Monument Creek, which he calls the forks of the Fontaine qui Bouille:

The road to Cherry Creek here leaves the Fontaine qui Bouille and bears to the right. There is a large

Indian trail which crosses the main creek and takes a northwesterly course towards Pike's Peak. By going up this trail about two miles, a mineral spring will be found which gives the stream its name of "The Fountain that Boils." This spring, or rather these springs, for there are two, both of which boil up out of the solid rock, are among the greatest natural curiosities that I have ever seen. The water is strongly impregnated with salts, but is delightful to the taste and somewhat similar to the Congress water. It will well compensate one for the trouble of visiting it.

Marcy claims that while waiting at the mouth of Cherry Creek for a ferry-boat to be constructed to take them over the Platte River, which was very high at the time, one of his employees washed a small amount of gold dust from the sands of Cherry Creek. This employee was discharged soon after and went direct to St. Louis, where he told of his discovery, and Marcy claims that this was the beginning of the mining excitement in the Pike's Peak region. This is different from other versions of the event, the most probable of which is that the discovery of gold was first made by the semi-civilized Cherokee Indians on their way to California.

What was known as the old Cherokee trail came up the Arkansas River to a point about twelve miles below the mouth of the Fontaine qui Bouille. From that place it ran in a northwesterly direction across the hills, striking that creek about eight or ten miles above its mouth; thence up the valley of the Fontaine to a point near the present town of Fountain; turning northerly by the way of Jimmy's Camp to the head of Cherry Creek, and down Cherry Creek to its mouth, where Denver now stands. From this place, after running northerly along the base of the mountains for a considerable distance, it struck across the mountains through Bridger's Pass, and then turned westerly along the usual traveled road to California. This trail was used by the first gold-seeking parties which came to the present State of Colorado in 1858. The first of these parties arrived at Cherry Creek only about two months after Marcy left. The second party followed a week or two later, and the third party, of which Anthony Bott, of Colorado City, was a member, was close behind it. Members of this third party explored the region around where Colorado City now stands, and later, with some others, returned and laid out the town.

In 1859, occurred the memorable visit of Horace Greeley to the Pike's Peak region. He arrived in Denver, June 16th, having come by the Smoky Hill route. Writing from Denver, he says, among other things:

I have been passing, meeting, observing, and trying to converse with Indians, almost ever since I crossed the Missouri River. Eastern Kansas is checkered with their reservations,—Delaware, Kaw, Ottawa, Osage, Kickapoo, Potawatamie, while the buffalo range and all this side belong to, and are parceled among the Cheyennes, the Arapahoes, and the Apaches, or perhaps among the two former only, as Indian boundaries are not well defined. At all events, we have met or passed bands of these three tribes, with occasional visitors from the Sioux on the north, and the Comanches on the south, all these tribes having for the present a good understanding. The Utes who inhabit the mountains are stronger and braver than any one of the three tribes first named, though hardly a match for them all, are at war with them. The Arapahoe Chief, Left Hand, assures me that his people were always at war with the Utes; at least he has no recollection, no tradition, of a time when they were at peace. Some two or three hundred lodges of Arapahoes are encamped in and about this log city, calculating that the presence of the whites will afford some protection to their wives and children against a Ute onslaught, while the braves are off on any of their fighting—that is stealing—expeditions. An equal or larger body of Utes are camped in the mountains some forty or fifty miles west, and the Arapahoe warriors recently returned in triumph from a war party on which they managed to steal about one hundred horses from the Utes, but were obliged to kill most of them in their rapid flight so that they only brought home forty more than they took away. They are going out again in a day or two, and have been for some days practicing secret incantations and public observances with reference thereto. Last midnight they were to have had a great war dance and to have left on the warpath to-day, but their men sent out after their horses reported that they saw three Utes on the plain, which was regarded as premonitory of an attack, and the braves stood to their arms all night and were very anxious for white aid in case of the Ute foray on their lodges here in Denver. Such an attack seems very improbable and I presume the three Utes who caused all this uproar were simply scouts or spies on the watch for just such marauding surprise parties as our Arapahoe neighbors are constantly meditating. I do not see why they need to take even this trouble. There are points on the mountain range west of this city, where a watchman with sharp eyes and a good glass could command the entire plain for fifty miles north, south, and east of him, and might hence give intelligence of any Arapahoe raid at least a day before a brave entered the mountains; for though it is true that Indians on the warpath travel or ride mainly by night, I find that the Arapahoes do this only after they have entered on what they consider disputed or dangerous ground; that they start from their lodges in open day and only advance under cover of darkness after they are within the shadows of the mountains. Hence the Utes, who are confessedly the stronger, might ambush and destroy any Arapahoe force that should venture into their Rocky Mountain recesses, by the help of a good spy-glass and a little "white forecast"; but the Indians are children. Their arts, wars, treaties, alliances, habitations, crafts, properties, commerce, comforts, all belong to the very lowest and rudest ages of human existence. Any band of schoolboys from ten to fifteen years of age are quite as capable of ruling their appetites, devising and upholding a public policy, constituting and conducting a state or community, as the average Indian tribe.

I have learned to appreciate better than hitherto, and to make more allowance for the dislike, aversion, and contempt wherewith Indians are usually regarded by their white neighbors, and have been since the days of the Puritans. It needs but little familiarity with the actual, palpable aborigines, to convince anyone that the poetical Indian—the Indian of Cooper and Longfellow—is only visible to the poet's eye.

The Utes seldom visited Colorado City and the region round about in the early days, except in the winter, which was the only time they could do so with a fair degree of safety. A majority of the tribe had been on friendly terms with the English-speaking people from the time of their earliest contact with that race. It is true that straggling bands of Utes occasionally committed acts of depredation, and such bands on one or two occasions killed white people, but these acts were not approved by the majority of the tribe.

One of these exceptions occurred on Christmas day, 1854, at Fort Napesta, on the present site of the city of Pueblo. It is said that the men who occupied the fort were celebrating the day with the liquid that both cheers and inebriates, and in the midst of their jollity, a band of wandering Utes came by and was invited to join in the revelry. The Indians, nothing loath, partook of the white man's Taos lightning, the product of a distillery at Taos, New Mexico, and the natural consequence was an attack upon the whites which resulted in all the latter being killed.

In 1866, a small band of Utes began a raid upon the settlers on Huerfano Creek, but when the news reached Ouray, the head chief of the tribe, he sent runners out at once to warn the settlers and then went to the scene of action with a band of his faithful warriors. He soon afterwards took the hostile Indians prisoners and compelled them to go to Fort Garland and remain there, in this manner quickly ending the trouble. Ouray was always the friend of the whites, and is entitled to the very greatest credit for the able manner in which he held the Utes under control up to the time of his death, in 1881.

Ouray was born at Taos, New Mexico, in 1833. His father was a Tabeguache Ute and his mother a Jicarilla Apache. His boyhood was passed among the better class of Mexicans, chiefly as a herder of sheep. He learned Spanish and always preferred it to his native tongue. When eighteen years of age, he joined the band of Utes of which his father was leader, then located in southwestern Colorado. From that time until about 1860, he led the life of a wild Indian, passing his time hunting in the mountains and on the plains, varied by an occasional battle with the hereditary enemies of his people, the Kiowas, Sioux, Cheyennes, and Arapahoes of the plains, in which he acquired the reputation of a courageous and skillful warrior. In 1859, he chose a wife, named Chipeta, from among the Tabaguache maidens, to whom he was always devotedly attached, and who bore him a son. This child was captured by the Cheyennes in 1863, they having surprised a hunting camp of Utes under Ouray's command, near the present site of Fort Lupton on the Platte River. The boy was never recovered and, indeed, was never heard of afterwards.

In person Ouray was of the almost invariably short stature which distinguishes his people from those of the plains tribes. He stood about five feet seven inches high and in his later years became quite portly. His head was strikingly large and well-shaped, his features were regular, bearing an expression of dignity in repose, but lighting up pleasantly in conversation. In his ordinary bearing his manner was courtly and gentle, and he was extremely fond of meeting and conversing with cultivated white men, with whom he was a genial companion, compelling their respect and favor by the broad enlightenment of his views. In his habits he was a model, never using tobacco, abhorring whiskey, and taking only a sip of wine when in company with those who were indulging, and then merely as a matter of courtesy to them. He never swore nor used obscene language, was a firm believer in the Christian religion, and about two years before his death united himself with the Methodist Church.

When in active command of his men, his word was law, and disobedience meant death. In the summer of 1874 at Bijou, while returning from Denver to their camp in the south, one of his men decided to build a fire and started to cut some wood for that purpose within the enclosure of a white settler. Ouray, discovering his intention, ordered him back, reminding him that they must not trespass upon the property of the white man. The obstinate Ute replied that he must have firewood and that he would cut it anyway. Ouray answered that if he did, he would kill him, whereat the other observed that two could play at that game. Instantly both started for their guns, reaching them at about the same time, but Ouray was quicker than his adversary and shot him.

Trails, Mineral Springs, Game 71

On another occasion he shot and broke the arm of Johnson, a member of his tribe, who afterwards caused much of the trouble at the White River Agency. Johnson was given to gambling, horseracing, lying, and trickery of all kinds. In the present case, he had stolen some horses from white men, and refused to return them when commanded to do so, thereby, in Ouray's opinion, bringing disgrace upon the Ute nation, for which he had to be punished.

In the foregoing, I have quoted freely from General Frank Hall's History of Colorado. General Hall had unusual opportunities for knowing Ouray and of his dealings with the whites.

It was through the prompt and decisive action of Ouray that the leaders of the massacre of Meeker and others at the White River Agency, in 1879, were surrendered to the authorities for punishment. The early settlers of Colorado owe to Ouray a debt of gratitude, and a monument to his memory should at some time be erected by the people of this State. Ouray frequently came to Colorado City in the early days, and sometimes his visits were of considerable duration.

In the winter of 1865–1866, a large body of Ute Indians camped for several months on the south side of the Fountain, opposite Colorado

City. On departing in the spring, they abandoned a squaw who had broken a leg, leaving her in a rudely constructed tent, or tepee. Had not the women of Colorado City taken her in charge she would have starved. After the Indians left, she was moved into a log cabin in Colorado City and provided with all she needed until her death, which occurred a few months later. The Utes seemed to think nothing of this heartless act, and even the abandoned squaw did not seem to resent it. It was a very common occurrence for the Indians of most of the tribes to abandon the aged and disabled, as in moving around, they did not wish to be burdened with those who were incapable of taking care of themselves.

In the winter of 1866–1867, a thousand or more Utes camped for several months below Manitou, between the Balanced Rock and the Fountain. Game was very scarce in this region during that winter and the Indians suffered for want of food. Finally, they reached such a strait that their chiefs made a demand upon the citizens of Colorado City for twenty sacks of flour, and intimated that unless it was produced forthwith, they would be compelled to march into town and take it by force. The citizens, realizing their utter helplessness in the matter, obtained the flour without delay and

Trails, Mineral Springs, Game

turned it over to the Indians. This was the only time in all the early period that Colorado City suffered from the presence of the Utes.

Chaveno and Colorow were the principal chiefs of this band. Chaveno was an Indian of a good deal of intelligence. When visiting the whites he always went about dressed in an army officer's uniform of dark blue which had been given him by an officer at Fort Garland. Chaveno was always strutting around, and seemed very proud of himself in his uniform, of which he took the greatest possible care. In the matter of dress, Colorow was the reverse. He seemed to have no liking whatever for the white man's costume. His physique was like that of Ouray, short, but of powerful build. He had been a noted warrior in his early days and delighted in telling of his exploits in the various battles with the Cheyennes and Arapahoes in which he had taken part. Colorow was treacherous by nature and his friendship for the whites was not always to be depended upon.

In the winter of 1874–1875, Ouray, with a band of six hundred Utes, camped at Florissant for several months. One day a Mr. Marksberry, living on Tarryall Creek, rode up to the Post Office at Florissant, tied his horse, and went into the building. The pony attracted the attention of an Indian named Antelope, who claimed the animal as his own; he slipped off the saddle and bridle, and, jumping on the pony's back, rode away. Marksberry and a friend, being determined to recover the pony, followed the band to their camp in Beaver Park, south of Pike's Peak. Marksberry found his pony with the Indian herd, caught it, and was turning away, when Antelope, hidden behind a tree, shot and instantly killed him. Chief Ouray, always ready to "travel the white man's road," gave up Antelope to justice. Upon trial of the case in the courts of Arapahoe County, some months later, he was acquitted.

The Utes, by treaties made in March, 1868, April, 1874, and March, 1880, ceded to the general government all the lands claimed by them within the boundaries of the present State of Colorado, except a small reservation retained for their own use in the southwestern part of the State.

CHAPTER III

THE INDIAN TROUBLES OF 1864

AS I have before mentioned, war parties of Cheyennes and Arapahoes continued to make occasional trips through the Ute Pass to the mountains in search of their enemies, the Utes, until 1864. As these war parties seldom tarried long in this vicinity, their presence was not seriously objected to during the first two or three years, but after rumors of impending trouble with them became current, their visits were looked upon with a good deal of apprehension. From the year 1859 to the beginning of 1863, the wagon trains that brought supplies from the Missouri River to Colorado came and went without molestation, but it was noticed, from the latter part of 1862 on, that the Indians of the plains were anxious to secure guns and ammunition, and were acquiring more than was necessary for their ordinary hunting. Early in 1863, they began to attack and rob wagon trains, steal horses, and threaten exposed settlements, but nothing occurred to cause any great alarm in the immediate Pike's Peak region, until the spring of 1864. During a very considerable portion of the next four years, however, the people of El Paso County experienced all the horrors of Indian warfare.

My story of the Indian troubles of that period will necessarily be much in the nature of a personal narrative. At the time hostilities began, I was little more than eighteen years old, and as fond of excitement and adventure as boys at that age usually are. I had a part in many of the occurrences which I shall mention, and was personally familiar with the details of most of the others.

About the 20th of June, 1864, word reached Colorado City that a day or two previously, the Hungate family, living on Running Creek about forty miles northeast of Colorado City, had been murdered by the Indians. The father and mother had been shot down and mutilated with horrible brutality, and the children who had tried to escape had been pursued and killed, so that not one of the family was left alive. This news made the people of Colorado City, and the settlers along the Fountain and on the Divide, very uneasy, and of course, after that, they were constantly on the lookout, not knowing where the savages might next appear.

Indian Troubles of 1864   77

Two or three weeks after the murder of the Hungate family, some cattle herders came into Colorado City late one evening and told of having seen near Austin's Bluff, a half a dozen mounted Indians who seemed to be acting mysteriously. Following the killing of the Hungate family, and other acts of hostility at various places on the plains, this was indeed alarming news. Consequently, early the following morning an armed party went to the place where the Indians had been seen, found their trail, and followed it. In this way it was discovered that, some time during the previous night, the Indians had been on the hill that overlooks Colorado City on the north, and that the trail from that point led into the mountains. The direction from which these Indians came, their mysterious movements after they were discovered, taken in connection with the recent acts of hostility, and the knowledge that the tribes of the plains had been attempting during the previous winter to make a coalition for the purpose of annihilating the settlements along the eastern base of the mountains, seemed convincing proof that this band was here for no good purpose.

At that time I was living with my father on the west side of Camp Creek, about half-way between Colorado City and the Garden of the Gods. I had been in town during the forenoon and had heard the alarming news, and as a result, after that father and I kept a sharp lookout for the savages. However, the day passed without anything further having been seen or heard of them. Shortly after sundown, my brothers Edgar and Frank, who were small boys, brought our cattle in from the neighborhood of the Garden of the Gods, and while I was helping to drive them into the corral adjacent to our house, I happened to look up the valley of Camp Creek, and there, about three-quarters of a mile away, I saw six mounted Indians leading an extra horse. They were going easterly along the old Indian trail, which I have heretofore described, that ran just south of the Garden of the Gods. As soon as I saw these Indians, I was sure that they were the party which had been trailed into Colorado City the night before. Without delay I strapped on a revolver, took my gun, and rode to Colorado City as fast as my pony could travel, to report what I had seen. The people had been greatly agitated during the day and, consequently, the news I brought caused much excitement.

It was at once decided that the Indians must be followed, and if possible the purpose of their visit ascertained. In less than three-quarters of an hour, ten mounted and well-armed men were ready for the pursuit. Those forming the party were Anthony Bott, Dr. Eggleston, William J. Baird, A. T. Cone, Ren Smith, myself, and four others whose names I cannot now recall. By a quarter of eight we were traveling along the trail taken by the Indians across the Mesa east of the Garden of the Gods. We appreciated the necessity of making as little noise as possible, and all talking was carried on in an undertone. The trail led from the Mesa down to Monument Creek, about a mile above the present site of Colorado Springs, and then crossed the stream over a bed of gravel that extended to the bluff on the eastern side. Thick clumps of willows enclosed the trail on both sides. It was a starlight night without clouds, but not light enough for us to see an object any distance away.

We suspected nothing, as we believed the Indians to be far ahead of us. But just as we came up on the first rise out of the willows on the east side of the creek we were startled to see them huddled together on the left of us, under the bank, apparently getting ready to start a small camp-fire, while to the right were their ponies, which had been turned out to graze. The Indians were just as much surprised as we were, and for an instant the situation was extremely tense. As we refrained from firing, the Indians, knowing that they were at a disadvantage in not being able to reach their ponies, evidently with the hope of making us believe that they were friendly, began calling out "How! How!" as Indians usually do on meeting the whites. We then questioned them, hoping to ascertain the object of their presence in this locality. Some of our people had a slight knowledge of Spanish, with which the Indians seemed somewhat conversant, and in this way and by signs, we told them that we were there only for the purpose of ascertaining their object in visiting this region, and not to do them harm; that if they could show that they were here for no hostile purpose, we would permit them to go on their way unmolested, but in order to establish this fact it would be necessary for them to go with us to Colorado City, where competent interpreters could be found, and meanwhile we should require them to give up their arms. They apparently assented to this proposition, and at once surrendered such of their arms as were in sight. Six of us then dismounted, and each took an Indian in charge while he was securing his pony. The Indian I had in charge was a tall, slim fellow, fully six feet in height and probably not much over twenty years of age. He appeared to take the situation quietly and I had no reason to apprehend any trouble with him. I allowed him to lead his pony to the camp, where he put on the saddle and bridle and mounted the animal, as all were permitted to do. We then formed the Indians in ranks of twos, placing a file of our men on each side of them, each white man having charge of the Indian next to him, which left two extra whites for the front and two to guard the rear. I was in charge of the Indian on the left side of the rear rank and had hold of his bridle with my right hand. The order was given to march and we started east towards the plateau on which Colorado Springs is now built. We had proceeded only eight or ten feet when the Indians suddenly halted. From the time they mounted they had been talking animatedly with one another in their own language. Just then someone happened to see that one of the Indians had a knife in his hand. This was taken from him and then we made a systematic search of the others and found that most of them had knives, and one a spear concealed under his blanket. It was with great difficulty that we twisted these weapons from their hands, but finally, as we thought, secured everything of that nature. The order was again given to march. Immediately following this, the Indians gave a tremendous warwhoop, shook their blankets, and were out from between us before we realized what was happening. The bridle rein in my hand was jerked away before I knew it. We were all so dazed that the Indians probably were seventy-five to one hundred feet away before our people began shooting. Meantime, my pony, which was of Indian breed, had become almost unmanageable. He seemed to be determined to go off with the other Indian ponies and I had the greatest difficulty in restraining him. Before I succeeded, I was so far in front that I was in great danger of being shot by our own people. By the time I could get my pony under control, the Indians were too far away for me to shoot with hope of doing any execution, but during this time the others had been making such good use of their weapons that in a few minutes the affair was over, and five of the Indians had fallen from their ponies. Whether they had been killed or wounded we did not know until some years later. We only knew that their ponies were running riderless over the plains. It was now about ten o'clock, and quite dark; consequently we made little effort to locate the dead and wounded. We rounded up the ponies, there being six of them, one a pack animal, and after gathering up such of the belong-

Indian Troubles of 1864

ings of the Indians as they had dropped in their flight, we started on our return to Colorado City.

The whole occurrence made one of the weirdest scenes that it has ever been my fortune to witness. First the sudden discovery of the Indians in the darkness of the night; the group formed of the Indians with the whites surrounding them; the mounting of the ponies; the shrill war-whoop of six savages ringing out in the solitude, followed by the shots, and then the riderless horses running hither and thither over the plain. The dramatic scene was completed a few minutes later by the rounding up of these riderless ponies and the beginning of the march back to Colorado City over the present town site of Colorado Springs, the only inhabitants of which at that time were the antelope and the coyotes. Our road led us over the present College reservation, down what is now Cascade Avenue to a ford crossing the Monument Creek, just west of the present Rio Grande freight station.

On the way home, the thought came to us whether we could have done differently under the circumstances. We knew the tribes to which these Indians belonged were at war with the whites, and that, unless they were on their way to fight the Utes, they were here on no peaceable errand so far as our people were concerned. Their course in going only to the foot of the mountains, showed that they were not seeking the Utes, and their actions under cover of the previous night, and afterward, up to the time they were captured, proved conclusively that they were here as scouts of a larger party, to ascertain and to report the strength of the town and its surrounding settlements. When first discovered, they were in an out-of-the-way spot, and from that time on until their capture, they traveled over abandoned roads and trails, probably hoping in this way to fulfill their mission without detection. These things convinced us that we had accomplished an important work, and the only regret we had was that we had not been able to bring the captives into town.

Early the following morning several of our party returned to the scene of the occurrence of the night before, hoping to find the bodies of the Indians who unquestionably had been killed in the mêlée, but there was nothing to indicate the struggle excepting a few articles of clothing and personal adornment, and marks upon the ground showing where the dead and wounded had evidently lain. Several years afterward, we learned from the Cheyennes that three of this scouting party had been killed outright, one was so seriously wounded that he died shortly afterward, another was slightly wounded, and one had escaped unhurt. The last, with the aid of the one slightly wounded, had carried off and buried the dead during the night.

News of our evening's experience spread rapidly and created intense excitement in Colorado City and throughout the county. The people of El Paso County now realized that they were face to face with Indian troubles of the most serious nature, and that arrangements for the defense of the town and surrounding country must immediately be made. The fighting strength of the Pike's Peak region was exceedingly limited, as compared with the great horde of savages that occupied our eastern frontier. Probably there were not over three hundred men of all ages in El Paso County at that time. And, as further showing the precarious position of the community, I wish to call attention to the fact that the frontier settlements of the United States at that time extended but little west of the Missouri River, leaving the narrow belt of settlements along the eastern base of the mountains in Colorado separated from the nearest communities to the east by a stretch of plains at least four hundred miles in width, inhabited only by wild and savage tribes of nomadic Indians. The same condition existed on the north to the

British possessions, and to the west the Ute Indians held undisputed sway to the Great Salt Lake valley. To the south, with the exception of a small part of New Mexico sparsely settled by feeble and widely scattered communities of Spanish-speaking people, wild tribes roamed over every portion of the country for hundreds of miles. From the foregoing, it will be seen that the settlements of Colorado were but a small island of civilization in a sea of savagery. Our settlements were at times completely cut off from civilization in every direction by this cordon of savage tribes; their very existence was now threatened, with no hope of assistance from the National Government, because of the civil war which was then at its most critical stage, demanding every resource of the nation. Threatened as they were by hordes of hostile savages and under conditions that would have had a disheartening effect upon a people not inured to frontier life, our settlers had no thought of allowing themselves to be driven out or overwhelmed.

Warning was at once sent to every family living down the Fountain and on the Divide, the result being that within a day or two almost every ranch in the county was abandoned. The people for fifteen miles down the valley below Colorado City

Indian Troubles of 1864

came to that town. Those living below gathered at the extreme lower edge of the county and there built a place of defense. In Colorado City the work of constructing a fort around an old log hotel was started at once. Green pine logs, ten to fifteen inches in diameter and about fifteen feet long, were cut on the adjacent mountains, brought in, and set in the ground close together, entirely surrounding the building, making a defensive structure about twelve feet high. At intervals through these logs portholes were made for use in repelling an attack. During the next month or two all the women and children of the town as well as those who had congregated there from the country slept at night in this fortification. Throughout this time a picket force of three or four mounted men was maintained night and day on the flat east of the town, and out on the present site of Colorado Springs. There was scarcely a day during this period in which Indians were not seen at various points in the country to the east of Colorado City, and on the borders of the settlements along the Fountain, but as the people everywhere were watchful, the savages had little opportunity of catching any one unawares.

About two weeks after the occurrence on Monument Creek, a messenger arrived at Colorado City, sent by Governor Evans to warn the people of an impending attack upon the settlements of the Territory by the Cheyennes, Arapahoes, and other hostile Indians. It appears that the Governor had received information from Elbridge Gerry, one of his secret agents, that eight hundred warriors belonging to the Cheyenne, Arapahoe, and other hostile Indian tribes, were in camp at the Point of Rocks near the head of Beaver Creek in eastern Colorado, and had planned a simultaneous attack upon the frontier settlements of Colorado extending from a point in the valley of the Platte River one hundred miles below Denver, to the Arkansas River at the mouth of the Fontaine qui Bouille. According to the program agreed upon by the Indians, one hundred warriors were to go to the valley of the Platte, two hundred and fifty to the head of Cherry Creek, and the remainder of the eight hundred to the valley of the Fountain and Arkansas rivers. On reaching the appointed localities, these parties were to be divided into small bands, each one of which was to attack a farmhouse, kill the occupants, loot the property, and run off the stock.

Elbridge Gerry, from whom the information of the proposed raid was received, was the grandson of a signer of the Declaration of Independence, and although an educated man, had lived with the Indians for a good many years and had married a Cheyenne woman. At this time, he was living with his Indian wife on a stock ranch in the valley of the Platte River, sixty to seventy miles below Denver. It was here that the information reached him, through two Cheyenne chiefs, who came to warn him of the impending danger. Gerry received the word about midnight and early next morning started on horseback for Denver to notify Governor Evans, arriving there about eleven o'clock that night, having ridden the sixty or seventy miles without resting. As the date set for the raid was but a day or two off, Governor Evans at once dispatched messengers in every direction to notify the people. The one sent to Colorado City reached that place the next afternoon, and warning was immediately sent by messengers to the few ranchmen down the Fountain and east of Colorado City, who for urgent reasons had been compelled temporarily to return to their homes.

The following day, small bands of Indians appeared along the entire frontier of El Paso County, but their raid was a failure, as the warnings given through the occurrence on Monument Creek, and that of the Governor, had put every one on guard; consequently the savages found that the settlers at every point had either fled, or were fully prepared to defend themselves.

That the information given by Gerry was absolutely correct, was shown by the fact that at the appointed time the Indians appeared along the entire frontier of Colorado, from the Platte to the Arkansas River. However, in almost every locality, as in El Paso County, they found the settlers on the lookout, consequently, the wholesale slaughter planned did not take place. After killing one man near Fort Lupton, below Denver, two or three near the head of Cherry Creek, and stealing many cattle, the larger part of the Indians returned to their rendezvous out on the plains, leaving a few warriors along the borders to harass the settlers during the remainder of the summer.

The Point of Rocks on Beaver Creek, where the eight hundred Indians were in camp, is about one hundred miles northeast of Colorado City. It is practically certain that the Indians we captured on Monument Creek two or three weeks previous were from that camp and had been sent out to secure information concerning the settlers of this region, preparatory to the raid they were then planning. There is every probability that an

Indian Troubles of 1864

awful calamity would have befallen the settlers of this county had not the discovery, capture, and escape of these scouts aroused our people to a full realization of their impending danger. Had the news brought by the messenger from the Governor been our first warning, it would have been impossible after his arrival to have brought any considerable portion of our scattered settlers into Colorado City before the appearance of the Indians.

Governor Evans, in telling of this incident in his evidence before the Committee on the Conduct of the War, in March, 1865, expressed the opinion that had the plan of the Indians been carried out without previous notice having been given to the settlers, it would have resulted in the most wholesale and extensive massacre that has ever been known. It was most fortunate for our people that timely notice was given in such an effective manner, because in those days news traveled slowly. Weekly mails were then the only method of disseminating news, as telegraph lines had not yet reached this part of the Territory, nor was there a newspaper published in the county; consequently news of Indian raids and outbreaks in other parts of the Territory often was a week or more in reaching El Paso County. Early realizing that they must depend upon their own resources, so far as I can see, the people of El Paso County took all necessary precautions, and acted wisely in every emergency.

One day early in September, 1864, a company of the First Colorado Cavalry on its way from one of the forts in New Mexico to Denver stopped for the noon meal at Jimmy's Camp, about ten miles east of Colorado City. Not having seen any Indians on the march, both officers and men were exceedingly skeptical as to there being any in this region, and had made sport of the settlers for being so unnecessarily alarmed. Upon making camp, the soldiers turned their horses, numbering from seventy-five to one hundred, out to graze, placing only one trooper in charge of them. The horses in their grazing gradually drifted farther and farther away from camp, until finally when they were almost half a mile distant, a band of Indians suddenly came tearing out of the timber just above and almost before the soldiers realized it they had rounded up the herd and were off over the hills, yelling back taunts as they rode away. The soldiers came marching into Colorado City on foot the next day, a dejected lot, and as they passed, it gave the settlers great pleasure to jeer at them.

CHAPTER IV

THE THIRD COLORADO AND THE BATTLE OF SAND CREEK

IT may be asked why we did not receive protection from the territorial authorities. The reason for this was that the Territory was without funds or a military organization. The Governor had repeatedly called the attention of the General Government to the helpless condition of our settlements, and asked that government troops be sent to protect them from the raids of the Indians; but at this time the entire military force of the nation was employed in suppressing the Rebellion, and little aid could be given. It is true that the companies of the First Regiment of Colorado Cavalry were distributed along the frontier, seldom more than one company in a place. Scattered in this way over a wide extent of country, they were of little or no use in the way of defense.

Meanwhile, the Indians were in virtual possession of the lines of travel to the east. Every coach that came through from the Missouri River to Denver had to run the gauntlet. Some were riddled with bullets, others were captured and their passengers killed. Instances were known where the victims were roasted alive, shot full of arrows, and subjected to every kind of cruelty the savages could devise. Finally, after many urgent appeals, the Governor of Colorado was permitted to organize a new regiment to be used in protecting the frontier settlements and in punishing the hostile Cheyennes and Arapahoes. The term of service was to be one hundred days; it was thought that by prompt action signal punishment could be inflicted on the savages in that time. Lieut. George L. Shoup, of the First Colorado, was commissioned as Colonel of the new regiment, which was designated as the Third Regiment of Colorado Volunteer Cavalry. Colonel Shoup had already proved himself to be a very able and efficient officer. He was afterward for many years United States Senator from the State of Idaho. From the day he received his appointment, he proceeded with great activity to organize his command. Recruiting officers had already been placed in almost every town in the Territory, and in less than thirty days eight or nine hundred men had been enlisted. Eight or ten others from El

Paso County besides myself joined the regiment at the first call. Among them were Anthony Bott, Robert Finley, Henry Coby, Samuel Murray, John Wolf, A. J. Templeton, Henry Miller, and a number of others whose names I do not now remember. The recruits from El Paso County were combined with those from Pueblo County and mustered in as Company G at Denver on the 29th day of August, 1864. Our officers were O. H. P. Baxter of Pueblo, Captain; Joseph Graham of the same county, First Lieutenant; and A. J. Templeton of El Paso County, Second Lieutenant. Within a short time after we had been mustered in at Denver, we marched back through El Paso County and south to a point on the Arkansas River, five miles east of Pueblo, where we remained for the next two months, waiting for our equipment. Meanwhile, we were being drilled and prepared for active military duty.

On the last day of October and the first day of November of that year there was a tremendous snow-storm all over the region along the eastern base of the Rocky Mountains. The snowfall at our camp was twenty inches in depth; at Colorado City it was over two feet on the level, and on the Divide still deeper. All supplies for the company had to be brought to our camp by teams, from the

Commissary Department at Denver. The depth of the snow now made this impossible; consequently, in a few days we were entirely out of food. As there seemed to be no hope of relief within the near future, our Captain instructed every one who had a home to go there and remain until further notice. Half a dozen of us from El Paso County started out the following morning before daylight, and tramped laboriously all day and well into the night through deep snow along the valley of the Fountain. For a portion of the way a wagon or two had gone over the road since the storm, making it so rough that walking along it was almost impossible. As a result, we were so tired by dusk that we would have traveled no farther could we have found a place where food and shelter were to be obtained; but it was eleven o'clock that night before we could get any accommodations at all, and by that time we were utterly exhausted. We resumed our tramp the next morning, but I was two days in reaching my home in Colorado City, twenty-five miles distant. Two weeks later we were notified by our Captain that provisions had been obtained and that we should return to camp at once. We had already been clothed in the light blue uniform then used by the cavalry branch of the United States Army. Soon after

The Battle of Sand Creek

our return to camp we received our equipment of arms, ammunition, and the necessary accouterments. The guns were old, out-of-date Austrian muskets of large bore with paper cartridges from which we had to bite off the end when loading. These guns sent a bullet rather viciously, but one could never tell where it would hit. A little later on, our horses arrived. They were a motley looking group, composed of every kind of an equine animal from a pony to a plow horse. The saddles and bridles were the same as were used in the cavalry service and were good of the kind. I had the misfortune to draw a rawboned, square-built old plow horse, upon which thereafter I spent a good many uncomfortable hours. If the order came to trot, followed by an order to gallop, I had to get him well underway on a trot and he would be going like the wind before I could bring him into the gallop. Meanwhile his rough trot would be shaking me to pieces. From what I have said, it will be seen that our equipment, as to arms and mounts, was of the poorest kind.

The main part of the regiment had been in camp near Denver during all this time. This inactivity had caused a great deal of complaint among the officers and enlisted men. For the most part, the regiment had been enlisted from the ranchmen, miners, and business men of the State, and it was the understanding that they were to be given immediate service against the hostile Indians. The delay was probably unavoidable, being caused by the inability of the Government to promptly furnish the necessary horses and equipment, as the animals had to be sent from east of the Missouri River. The horses and equipment were received about the middle of November. A few days later, under command of Colonel Shoup, the main part of the regiment, together with three companies of the First Colorado, started on its way south, towards a destination known only to the principal officers. The combined force was under command of Col. John M. Chivington, commander of the military district of Colorado. The company to which I belonged joined the regiment as it passed our camp, about the 25th of November, and from that time on our real hardships began. We marched steadily down the valley of the Arkansas River, going into camp at seven or eight o'clock every night, and by the time we had eaten supper and had taken care of our horses, it was after ten o'clock. We were called out at four o'clock the next morning and were on the move before daylight. In order that no news of our march should be carried to the Indians, every man we met on

The Battle of Sand Creek

the road was taken in charge, and, for the same purpose, guards were placed at every ranch.

About four o'clock in the evening of November 28th, we arrived at Fort Lyon, to the great surprise of its garrison. No one at the fort even knew that the regiment had left the vicinity of Denver. A picket guard was thrown around the fort to turn away any Indians that might be coming in, and also to prevent any of the trappers or Indian traders who generally hung around there from notifying the savages of our presence.

Soon after our arrival at camp, we were told that the wagon train would be left behind at this point, and each man was instructed to secure from the commissary two or three pounds of raw bacon and sufficient "hardtack" to last three or four days, which he was to carry in his saddlebags. At eight o'clock that night, the regiment took up its line of march across the prairie, in a direction almost due north from Fort Lyon. Each company was formed into fours, and we pushed on rapidly. All night long it was walk, trot, gallop, dismount and lead. I had had very little sleep for two or three nights previously, and, consequently, this all-night march was very exhausting. During the latter part of the night, I would willingly have run the risk of being scalped by the Indians for a half-hour's sleep. Some time after midnight, our guide, intentionally as we thought, led us through one of the shallow lakes that are so plentiful on the plains of that region. He was understood to be more friendly to the Indians than to the whites, and perhaps he hoped our ammunition would get wet, and thus become ineffective in the anticipated engagement. During the night, in order to keep awake, we had been nibbling on our hardtack, which in the morning, much to our disgust, we found to be very much alive.

It was a bright, clear, starlight night; the air was crisp and uncomfortably cool, as might be expected at that time of year. Just as the sun was coming up over the eastern hills, we reached the top of a ridge, and away off in the valley to the northwest we saw a great number of Indian tents, forming a village of unusual size. We knew at once that this village was our objective point. Off to the left, between us and the village, was a large number of Indian ponies.

Two or three minutes later, orders came directing our battalion to capture the herd. Under command of a Major of the regiment, we immediately started on the run in order to get between the ponies and the Indian camp before our presence was discovered. We had not proceeded

The Battle of Sand Creek

any great distance before we saw half a dozen Indians coming toward the herd from the direction of the camp, but, on seeing our large force, they hesitated a moment and then started back as fast as their ponies could take them. We were not long in securing the herd, which consisted of between five and six hundred ponies. The officer in command placed from twenty to thirty men in charge of the ponies, with instructions to drive them away to some point where they would be in no danger of recapture. The remainder of the battalion then started directly for the Indian camp, which lay over a little ridge to the north of us. Meanwhile, the main part of the command had marched at a rapid rate down the slope to Sand Creek, along the northern bank of which the Indian camp was located. Crossing the creek some distance to the eastward of the village, they marched rapidly westward along the north bank until near the Indian village, where they halted, and the battle began. At the same time our battalion was coming in from the south. This left an opening for the Indians to the westward, up the valley of Sand Creek, and also to the northward, across the hills towards the Smoky Hill River. Before our battalion had crossed the low ridge which cut off the view of the village at the point where we captured the ponies, and had come in sight of the village again, the firing had become general, and it made some of us, myself among the number, feel pretty queer. I am sure, speaking for myself, if I hadn't been too proud, I should have stayed out of the fight altogether.

When we first came in sight of the Indian camp there were a good many ponies not far away to the north of it, and now when we came in sight of the camp again, after we had captured the other herd, we saw large numbers of Indians, presumably squaws and children, hurrying northward on these ponies, out of the way of danger. After the engagement commenced, the Indian warriors concentrated along Sand Creek, using the high banks on either side as a means of defense. At this point, Sand Creek was about two hundred yards wide, the banks on each side being almost perpendicular and from six to twelve feet high. The engagement extended along this creek for three or four miles from the Indian encampment. Our capture of the ponies placed the Indians at a great disadvantage, for the reason that an Indian is not accustomed to fighting on foot. They were very nearly equal to us in numbers, and had they been mounted, we should

The Battle of Sand Creek 103

have had great difficulty in defeating them, as they were better armed than we were, and their ponies were much superior for military purposes to the horses of our command.

From the beginning of the engagement our battery did effective work, its shells, as a rule, keeping the Indians from concentrating in considerable numbers at any one point. However, at one place, soon after getting into the fight, I saw a line of fifty to one hundred Indians receive a charge from one of our companies as steadily as veterans, and their shooting was so effective that our men were forced to fall back. Returning to the charge soon after, the troopers forced the Indians to retire behind the banks of the creek, which they did, however, in a very leisurely manner, leaving a large number of their dead upon the field. Our own company, Company G, became disorganized early in the fight, as did many of the other companies, and after that fought in little groups wherever it seemed that they could be most effective. After the first few shots, I had no fear whatever, nor did I see any others displaying the least concern as to their own safety. The fight soon became general all up and down the valley, the Indians continuously firing from their places of defense along the banks, and a constant fusillade being kept up by the soldiers, who were shooting at every Indian that appeared. I think it was in this way that a good many of the squaws were killed. It was utterly impossible, at a distance of two hundred yards, to discern between the sexes, on account of their similarity of dress.

As our detachment moved up the valley, we frequently came in line of the firing, and the bullets whizzed past us rather unpleasantly, but fortunately none of us was hurt. At one point we ran across a wounded man, a former resident of El Paso County, but then a member of a company from another county. A short time previously, as he passed too near the bank, a squaw had shot an arrow into his shoulder, inflicting a very painful wound. He was being cared for by the members of his own company. A little farther up the creek we crossed over to the north side, and then moved leisurely up the valley, shooting at the Indians whenever any were in sight. By this time, most of them had burrowed into the soft sand of the banks, which formed a place of defense for them from which they could shoot at the whites, while only slightly exposing themselves.

Soon after, we joined a detachment which was

carrying on a brisk engagement with a considerable force of Indians, some of whom were hidden behind one of the many large piles of driftwood along the banks of Sand Creek, while others were sheltered behind a similar pile in the center of the creek, which was unusually wide at that point. Our men were posted in a little depression just back from the north bank, from which some of them had crawled forward as far as they dared go, and were shooting into the driftwood, in the hope of driving the Indians from cover. Soon after I reached this point, a member of the company from Boulder, who had stepped out a little too far, and then turned around to speak to one of us, was shot in the back, the bullet going straight through his lungs and chest. Realizing at once that he was badly wounded, probably fatally so, he asked to be taken to his company. I volunteered to accompany him and, after helping him on his horse, we started across the prairie to where his company was supposed to be. With every breath, bubbles of blood were coming from his lungs and I had little hope that he would reach his comrades alive. Just as we reached the company, he fainted and was caught by his captain as he was falling from his horse. I returned immediately to the place that I had left and found the battle still going on. During my absence, our little force had been considerably increased by soldiers from other parts of the battlefield. It was now decided to make it so hot for the savages by continuous firing, that they would be compelled to leave their places of cover. Soon two or three of the Indians exposed themselves and were instantly shot down. In a short time, the remainder started across the creek towards its southern bank. They ran in a zigzag manner, jumping from one side to the other, evidently hoping by so doing that we would be unable to hit them, but by taking deliberate aim, we dropped every one before they reached the other bank.

About this time, orders came from the commanding officer directing us to return at once to the Indian camp, as information had been received that a large force of Indians was coming from the Smoky Hill River to attack us. Obeying this order, we marched leisurely down the creek, and as we went we were repeatedly fired at by Indians hidden in the banks in the manner I have described heretofore. We returned the fire, but the savages were so well protected that we had no reason to think any of our shots had proved effective. At one place, an Indian child, three or four years of age, ran out to us, holding up its hands and crying piteously. From its actions we inferred that it wished to be taken up. At first I was inclined to do so, but changed my mind when it occurred to me that I should have no means of taking care of the little fellow. We knew that there were Indians concealed within a couple of hundred yards of where we were, who certainly would take care of him as soon as we were out of the way; consequently we left him to be cared for by his own people. Every one of our party expressed sympathy for the little fellow, and no one dreamed of harming him.

As we neared the Indian camp, we passed the place where the severest fighting had occurred earlier in the day, and here we saw many dead Indians, a few of whom were squaws. At the edge of the camp, we came upon our own dead who had been brought in and placed in a row. There were ten of them, and we were informed that there were forty wounded in a hospital improvised for the occasion. Among the dead I expected to find the Boulder man whom I had taken to his company, but, strange to relate, he survived his wound, and I saw him two or three years afterwards, apparently entirely recovered. The number of our dead and wounded showed that the Indians had offered a vigorous defense, and as I have before stated, if they had been mounted, it is questionable whether the result would have been the same—had they remained to fight.

We reached the Indian camp about four o'clock in the afternoon, the battle having continued without cessation from early morning until that time. The companies were immediately placed in position to form a hollow square, inside of which our horses were picketed. I was so utterly exhausted for want of sleep and food, as were many others of our company, that I hunted up a buffalo robe, of which there were large numbers scattered around, threw myself down on it, and was asleep almost as soon as I touched the ground. The next thing I remember was being awakened for supper, about dusk. We were told that we must sleep with our guns in our hands, ready for use at any moment. Near midnight, we were awakened by a more than vigorous call of our officers, ordering us to fall into line immediately to repel an attack. We rushed out, but in our sleepy condition had difficulty in forming a line, as we hardly knew what we were doing. In the evening, by order of the commanding officer, all the Indian tents outside of our encampment had been set on fire and now were blazing brightly all around us.

The Battle of Sand Creek

We heard occasional shots in various directions, and in the light of the fire saw what looked to be hundreds of Indian ponies running hither and thither. We saw no Indians, but we knew that savages in an encounter always lie on the side of their ponies opposite from the enemies they are attacking. From the number of what seemed to be horses that could be seen in every direction, we thought that we should surely be overwhelmed. After forming in line, and while waiting for the attack, we discovered that what in our sleepy condition we had imagined to be ponies, was nothing but the numerous dogs of the Indian camp, which, having lost their masters, were running wildly in every direction. Nevertheless, it was evident that Indians were all around us, as our pickets had been fired upon and driven in from every side of the camp. After remaining in line for a considerable length of time, without being attacked, the regiment was divided into two divisions, one of which was marched fifty feet in front of the other. We were then instructed to get our blankets, and, wrapping ourselves in them, with our guns handy, we lay down and slept the remainder of the night.

In the Indian camp we found an abundance of flour, sugar, bacon, coffee, and other articles of food, sufficient for our maintenance, had we needed it, for a time. In many of the tents there were articles of wearing apparel and other things that had been taken from wagon-trains which the Indians had robbed during the previous summer. In these same tents we found a dozen or more scalps of white people, some of them being from the heads of women and children, as was evidenced by the color and fineness of the hair, which could not be mistaken for that of any other race. One of the scalps showed plainly from its condition that it had been taken only recently. Certain members of our regiment found horses and mules in the Indian herd that had been stolen from them by the hostiles in their various raids during the preceding year. The camp was overflowing with proof that these Indians were among those who had been raiding the settlements of Colorado during the previous summer, killing people, robbing wagon-trains, burning houses, running off stock, and committing outrages of which only a savage could be guilty; this evidence only corroborated in the strongest possible manner what we already knew. Among the members of our regiment, there were many who had had friends and relatives killed, scalped, and mutilated by these Indians, and almost every man had

The Battle of Sand Creek

sustained financial loss by reason of their raids; consequently it is not surprising they should be determined to inflict such punishment upon the savages as would deter them from further raids upon our settlements. Notwithstanding the fact that this grim determination was firmly fixed in the mind of every one, I never saw any one deliberately shoot at a squaw, nor do I believe that any children were intentionally killed.

About noon of the day following the battle, our wagon-train came up, and was formed into a hollow square in the center of our camp, the lines being drawn in, so that if necessary the wagons could be used as a means of defense. We knew that on the Smoky Hill River, from fifty to seventy-five miles distant, there was another large body of Cheyennes and Arapahoes which might attack us at any time. In every direction throughout the day, many Indians were seen hovering around our camp. Scouting parties were seldom able to get very far away from camp without being fired upon, and several of our men were killed and a number wounded in the skirmishes that took place. During the second night of our stay on the battle ground, we were kept in line continuously, with our arms ready for use at a moment's notice. At intervals during the entire night, there was an exchange of shots at various points around the camp.

I never understood why we did not follow up our victory by an attack upon the hostile bands camped on the Smoky Hill River, but I assume it was on account of our regiment's inferior horses, arms, and equipment. Probably Colonel Chivington, taking this into consideration, thought his force not strong enough to fight such a large party successfully.

The following day, the command took up its line of march down the Big Sandy and followed it to the Arkansas River, then easterly, along the north side of that stream to the western boundary of Kansas. Soon after we reached the Arkansas River, we found the trail of a large party of Indians traveling down the valley. They seemed to be in great haste to get away from us, as they had thrown away their camp kettles, buffalo robes, and everything that might impede their flight. Realizing that the Indians could not be overtaken with the whole command, on account of the poor condition of many of the horses, our officers specially detailed three hundred of our best mounted and best armed men, and sent them forward in pursuit under forced march; but even this plan was unsuccessful, and the pursuit was

The Battle of Sand Creek 113

finally abandoned when near the Kansas line. The term of enlistment of our regiment had already expired, for which reason the command was reluctantly faced about, and the return march to Denver begun.

From the time we left the Sand Creek battle ground, it had been very cold and disagreeable. Sharp, piercing winds blew from the north almost incessantly, making us extremely uncomfortable during the day, and even more so at night. Being without tents and compelled to sleep on the open prairie, with no protection whatever from the wind, at times we found the cold almost unbearable. The thin, shoddy government blankets afforded only the slightest possible protection against the bitter winds; consequently those were fortunate indeed who could find a gully in which to make their bed. Our march back to Denver was leisurely and uneventful. We reached there in due course and were mustered out of service on the 29th day of December, 1864. We dispersed to our homes, convinced that we had done a good work and that it needed only a little further punishment of the savages permanently to settle the Indian troubles so far as this Territory was concerned.

CHAPTER V

A DEFENSE OF THE BATTLE OF SAND CREEK

FEW events in American history have been the subject of so much misrepresentation as the battle of Sand Creek. It has gone down into history as an indefensible massacre of peaceable Indians, and perhaps nothing that can now be said will change this erroneous impression of the world at large, notwithstanding the fact that the accusation is unjust and a libel upon the people of Colorado. Worst of all, it was given wide publicity through the reports of two Congressional committees following unfair, one-sided, and prejudiced investigations. Unfortunately, at that time, Colorado, being a Territory, had no Senators or Representatives in Congress to defend the good name of its people, and to add to the bad features of the situation, its people at home realized but dimly what was taking place at Washington, until after the mischief was done; consequently to a great extent the Congressional investigations went by default, so far as the people of Colorado were concerned.

It should be kept in mind that Colorado, comparatively speaking, was more remote from the rest of the world at that time than Alaska is to-day, and the means of disseminating news throughout the Territory were exceedingly limited. From early in November of 1864 until March, 1865, the coaches that carried the mail between the Missouri River towns and Denver ceased running on account of the hostility of the Indians, and all this time Colorado was cut off from the rest of the world, except for a limited telegraph service that did not reach any point in the Territory outside of Denver. Consequently, the enemies of Colonel Chivington and the Third Colorado Cavalry, had full sway in their efforts to blacken the reputation of these representative citizens of Colorado. I wish to emphasize the fact that a large majority of the members of the Third Colorado Cavalry were high-class men, whatever may be said to the contrary. Colorado had been settled less than six years and most of its inhabitants had come to the Territory in 1860, only four years previously. These people were from every part of the United States, many of them farmers, merchants, and professional men, and the men who enlisted in the Third Colorado were largely of this class.

The accusations on which the various Congressional and military investigations were based had their origin in the jealousy of military officers. It was the same kind of spirit that caused the loss of more than one battle in the Civil War. However, at Sand Creek, on account of the secrecy of preparations, the victory could not be prevented, but the good effects could be, and were, completely nullified, to the great detriment of the people of Colorado; and this was done by officers who had been former residents of the Territory and were indebted to it for their official positions. But fully to understand the animus of these officers, it is necessary for the reader to know something of their personality, as well as that of the other officers involved in the controversy.

Colonel John M. Chivington, who was in command at the battle of Sand Creek, and who was the principal target throughout the various investigations, was the Rev. John M. Chivington, who from 1860 to 1862 was in charge of the Methodist missions in the region now forming the State of Colorado. He was a member of the Kansas-Nebraska Conference, and had been selected for this mission work because of his

John M. Chivington
Colonel First Colorado Volunteer Cavalry

The Battle of Sand Creek   117

unusual energy, ability, and force of character. The commanding position that the Methodist Church early assumed in the Territory under his administration confirmed the wisdom of his appointment.

Upon the organization of the First Colorado Volunteer Cavalry in the early part of 1862, Mr. Chivington resigned his position as presiding elder of the Rocky Mountain District, and was commissioned Major of the new regiment. He at once became the regiment's most influential officer. He was the most prominent figure in its wonderful march to New Mexico, and the remarkable victories won by it over the invading Confederates were largely due to his brilliant leadership. By the end of the active campaign, which was a short one, Major Chivington had become so popular with the officers and enlisted men that upon the resignation of John P. Slough, the Colonel of the regiment, soon after, he was promoted to that position over Lieutenant-Colonel Samuel F. Tappan on petition of every commissioned officer of the regiment. Here was the beginning of all his troubles, as will be seen farther along in my narrative. Later, Colonel Chivington was appointed by General Canby to the command of the military district of Southern

New Mexico, and was afterward transferred to the command of the military district of Colorado, which position he held at the time of the battle of Sand Creek.

Colonel Chivington was a man of commanding personality, and possessed marked ability both as a preacher and as an army officer. I can do no better than quote what General Frank Hall says of him in his *History of Colorado:*

> Though wholly unskilled in the science of war, with but little knowledge of drill and discipline, Major Chivington, of Herculean frame and gigantic stature, possessed the courage and exhibited the discreet boldness, dash, and brilliancy in action which distinguished the more illustrious of our volunteer officers during the war. His first encounter with the Texans at Apache Cañon was sudden and more or less of a surprise. The occasion demanded not only instantaneous action, but such disposition of his force as to render it most effective against superior numbers and the highly advantageous position of the enemy. He seemed to comprehend at a glance the necessities of the situation and handled his troops like a veteran. His daring and rapid movement across the mountains and the total destruction of the enemy's train, simultaneously with the battle of Pigeon's Ranch, again attested his excellent generalship. It put an end to the war by forcing the invaders to a precipitate flight back to their homes. He hesitated at nothing. Sure of the devotion and

The Battle of Sand Creek 119

gallantry of his men, he was always ready for any adventure, however desperate, which promised the discomfiture of his adversaries.

We cannot but believe that had his application for the transfer of his regiment to the Army of the Potomac, or to any of the great armies operating under Grant, been acceded to, he would have made a still prouder record for himself, the regiment, and the Territory. That he was endowed with the capabilities of a superior commander, none who saw him in action will deny.

I fully concur in General Hall's estimate of Colonel Chivington's marked ability. I knew him well, as he was a frequent visitor at our house in the mining town of Hamilton, in the early days. The overshadowing reputation made by Colonel Chivington in the campaign against the Texas invaders of New Mexico, and his subsequent promotion to the colonelcy of the regiment over Lieutenant-Colonel Samuel F. Tappan, although apparently acquiesced in at the time, aroused a spirit of jealousy, envy, and antagonism against him on the part of a small group of officers headed by Lieutenant-Colonel Tappan and Major E. W. Wynkoop, which was participated in by Captain Soule, Lieutenant Cramer, and other subordinates. This antagonism manifested itself on every later occasion. It was the jealousy of mediocrity manifested against superior ability and worth; for one can search the records of the First Colorado in vain for anything noteworthy ever accomplished by either Tappan, Wynkoop, or Soule. After their return from New Mexico, these officers never allowed an opportunity to pass for discrediting and injuring the "Preacher Colonel," and after the battle of Sand Creek they never tired of referring to it as an evidence of his unfitness.

Lieutenant-Colonel Tappan had been a professional newspaper correspondent before entering the army, consequently, he had no trouble in filling the Eastern publications with exaggerated and distorted accounts of the battle. In his crusade he had the active aid of Major Wynkoop, of S. G. Colley, the Indian agent at Fort Lyon, and of all the Indian traders, interpreters, half-breeds, and others of similar character congregated around the Indian agency. He also had the support of the Indian Bureau at Washington, which usually took the sentimental side of every question affecting the Indians.

Prior to 1864 Indians who had been on the warpath during the summer were permitted to make peace in the fall, remain unmolested during the winter, receive annuities, rest up, and accumulate ammunition for the coming summer's raids; but

The Battle of Sand Creek 121

in that year the overtures of the Cheyennes and Arapahoes were rejected, except upon the condition that they deliver up their arms and submit to the military authorities. This they not only refused to do, but continued their depredations at places convenient to their winter camps, and received from Colonel Chivington's command the punishment they so richly deserved. Naturally this meant great financial loss to the Indian agents, traders, and hangers-on around the Indian agency; and, as a result, these people actively joined in the attack upon Colonel Chivington.

This crusade resulted in two Congressional investigations of the battle, and also in a hearing by a military commission. Before the Joint Special Committee of the two Houses of Congress the principal witnesses were Major Wynkoop, Captain Soule, Lieutenant Cramer, two Indian agents, two Indian traders, two half-breeds, and one interpreter to sustain the accusations, and only Governor Evans and three minor officers of the Third Colorado regiment for the defense. Aside from Governor Evans and the three minor officers just mentioned, the witnesses were extremely hostile to Colonel Chivington and were ready to go to any length in their testimony in order to blacken his reputation and that of the Third Colorado. In the investigation before the Joint Special Committee, neither Colonel Chivington nor Colonel Shoup was present or represented in any way. In the hearing before the Committee on the Conduct of the War, Colonel Shoup was not represented, and Colonel Chivington only by means of a deposition. As a result of these partial and one-sided investigations, both committees condemned Chivington and pronounced the battle a massacre. The most unjust and absurd investigation of all was that made by the military commission, which was composed of three officers of the First Colorado Cavalry, all subordinates of Colonel Chivington, headed by his inveterate enemy Lieutenant-Colonel Samuel F. Tappan.

The accusation made at each hearing was that the Cheyenne and Arapahoe Indians attacked by Colonel Chivington's command at Sand Creek were not only friendly to the whites, but were under the protection of the military authorities at Fort Lyon, and that the battle was, by the consent, if not by the direction of Colonel Chivington, an indiscriminate massacre. All of this I believe is proved to be untrue, to the satisfaction of any reasonable person, by the facts related in my account of the battle, and of the hostilities

Hon. John Evans
Governor of Colorado, 1862–1865

in El Paso County and elsewhere preceding it. In corroboration of my statements as to the hostile character of the Indians punished at Sand Creek, and to show the conditions existing elsewhere in the Territory previous thereto, I quote from Governor Evans's reply to the report of the Committee on the Conduct of the War, dated August 6, 1865.

In the Territorial days of Colorado, the Governor was ex-officio Superintendent of Indian Affairs. At the time of the Sand Creek battle, the Hon. John Evans, formerly of Illinois, was Governor of Colorado, and had held that office since the spring of 1862. Governor Evans was a personal friend of President Lincoln, and had been appointed Governor because of his high character, great ability, and efficiency in administrative affairs. Governor Evans's supervision of Indian affairs in Colorado during 1862, 1863, and 1864 made him a better qualified witness as to the conditions existing among the various tribes during these years than any man living. The following extracts from his reply to that part of the report of the Committee on the Conduct of the War, which, under the heading, "Massacre of the Cheyenne Indians," refers to his responsibility in the matter, tells of the attitude of the

Indians towards the whites during that period and of his own strenuous efforts to avert hostilities.

Executive Department and Superintendency of Indian Affairs, C. T.

Denver, August 6, 1865.

To the Public:

I have just seen, for the first time, a copy of the report of the Committee on the Conduct of the War, headed, " Massacre of Cheyenne Indians."

As it does me great injustice, and by its partial, unfair, and erroneous statements will mislead the public, I respectfully ask a suspension of opinion in my case until I shall have time to present the facts to said committee or some equally high authority, and ask a correction. In the meantime, I desire to lay a few facts before the public. The report begins:

"In the summer of 1864 Governor Evans, of Colorado Territory, as acting Superintendent of Indian Affairs, sent notice to the various bands and tribes of Indians within his jurisdiction, that such as desired to be considered friendly to the whites should repair to the nearest military post in order to be protected from the soldiers who were to take the field against the hostile Indians."

This statement is true as to such notice having been sent, but conveys the false impression that it was at the beginning of hostilities, and the declaration of war. The truth is, it was issued by authority of the Indian Department months after the war had become general, for the purpose of inducing the Indians to

The Battle of Sand Creek 125

cease hostilities, and to protect those who had been, or would become, friendly from the inevitable dangers to which they were exposed. This "notice" may be found published in the report of the Commissioner of Indian Affairs for 1864, page 218.

The report continues :

"About the close of the summer some Cheyenne Indians, in the neighborhood of the Smoky Hill, sent word to Major Wynkoop, commanding at Fort Lyon, that they had in their possession, and were willing to deliver up, some white captives they had purchased of other Indians. Major Wynkoop, with a force of over one hundred men, visited these Indians and recovered the white captives. On his return he was accompanied by a number of the chiefs and leading men of the Indians, whom he had brought to visit Denver for the purpose of conferring with the authorities there in regard to keeping the peace. Among them were Black Kettle and White Antelope, of the Cheyennes, and some chiefs of the Arapahoes. The council was held, and these chiefs stated that they were friendly to the whites and always had been."

Again they say :

"All the testimony goes to show that the Indians under the immediate control of Black Kettle and White Antelope, of the Cheyennes, and Left Hand of the Arapahoes, were, and had always been, friendly to the whites, and had not been guilty of any acts of hostility or depredations."

This word, which the committee say was sent to Major Wynkoop, was a letter to United States Indian Agent, Major Colley, which is published in the report of the Commissioner of Indian Affairs for 1865, page 233, and is as follows:

"CHEYENNE VILLAGE, August 29, 1864.

"MAJOR COLLEY:

"We received a letter from Bent wishing us to make peace. We held a council in regard to it. All come to the conclusion to make peace with you, providing you make peace with the Kiowas, Comanches, Arapahoes, Apaches, and Sioux. We are going to send a messenger to the Kiowas and to the other nations about our going to make peace with you. We heard that you have some [prisoners] in Denver. We have seven prisoners of yours which we are willing to give up, providing you give up yours. There are three war parties out yet, and two of Arapahoes. They have been out some time, and expected in soon. When we held this council there were few Arapahoes and Sioux present.

"We want true news from you in return. This is a letter.

"BLACK KETTLE and the other Chiefs."

Compare the above extract from the report of the committee with this published letter of Black Kettle, and the admission of the Indians in the council at Denver.

The committee say the prisoners proposed to be delivered up were *purchased of other Indians.* Black Kettle, in his letter, says: "We have seven prisoners of yours, which we are willing to give up, providing you give up yours." They say nothing about prisoners whom they had *purchased.* On the other hand, in the council held in Denver, Black Kettle said:

"Major Wynkoop was kind enough to receive the letter and visited them in camp, to whom they delivered four white prisoners, one other (Mrs. Snyder) having killed herself; that there are two women and one child yet in their camp whom they will deliver up as soon as they can get them in; Laura Roper, 16 or 17 years; Ambrose Asher, 7 or 8 years; Daniel Marble, 7 or 8 years; Isabel Ubanks, 4 or 5 years. The prisoners still with them [are] Mrs. Ubanks and babe, and a Mrs. Norton who was taken on the Platte. Mrs. Snyder is the name of the woman who hung herself. The boys were taken between Fort Kearney and the Blue."

Again: They did not deny having captured the prisoners, when I told them that having the prisoners in their possession was evidence of their having committed the depredations when they were taken. But White Antelope said: "We (the Cheyennes) took two prisoners west of Kearney, and destroyed the trains." Had they *purchased* the prisoners, they would not have been slow to make it known in this council.

The committee say the chiefs went to Denver to confer with the authorities about *keeping the peace.* Black Kettle says: "All come to the conclusion to *make peace* with you providing you will *make peace* with the Kiowas, Comanches, Arapahoes, Apaches, and Sioux."

Again the committee say:

"All the testimony goes to show that the Indians under the immediate control of Black Kettle and White Antelope, of the Cheyennes, and Left Hand, of the Arapahoes, *were, and had been friendly to the whites, and had not been guilty of any acts of hostility or depredations.*"

Black Kettle says in his letter: "We received a letter from Bent, wishing us to make peace." Why did Bent send a letter to *friendly* Indians, and want to make peace with Indians *who had always been friendly?* Again they say: "We have held a council in regard to it." Why did they hold a council in regard to making peace, when they were already peaceable? Again they say: "All come to the conclusion to *make peace* with you *providing* you make peace with the Kiowas, Comanches, Arapahoes, Apaches, and Sioux. We have seven prisoners of yours, which we are willing to give up, providing you give up yours. There are three *war* [not *peace*] *parties* out yet, and two of Arapahoes."

Every line of this letter shows that they were and had been at war. I desire to throw additional light upon this assertion of the committee that these Indians "were and had been friendly to the whites, and had not been guilty of any acts of hostility or depredations"; for it is upon this point that the committee accuses me of prevarication.

In the council held at Denver, White Antelope said: "We [the Cheyennes] took two prisoners west of Kearney and destroyed the trains." This was one of the most destructive and bloody raids of the war. Again, Neva (Left Hand's brother) said: "The Comanches, Kiowas, and Sioux have done much more harm than we have."

The entire report of this council shows that the Indians had been at war, and had been "guilty of acts of hostility and depredations."

As showing more fully the status and disposition of these Indians, I call your attention to the following extract from the report of Major Wynkoop, published in the report of the Commissioner of Indian Affairs for 1864, page 234, and a letter from Major Colley, their agent; same report, page 230. Also statement of Robert North; same report, page 224:

"FORT LYON, COLORADO, Sept. 18, 1864.

"SIR:
" . . . Taking with me under strict guard the Indians I had in my possession, I reached my destination and was confronted by from six to eight hundred Indian warriors, drawn up in line of battle and prepared to fight.

"Putting on as bold a front as I could under the circumstances I formed my command in as good order as possible for the purpose of acting on the offensive or defensive, as might be necessary, and advanced towards them, at the same time sending forward one of the Indians I had with me, as an emissary, to state that I had come for the purpose of holding a consultation with the chiefs of the Arapahoes and Cheyennes, to come to an understanding which might result in mutual benefit; that I had not come desiring strife, but was prepared for it if necessary, and advised them to listen to what I had to say, previous to making any more warlike demonstrations.

"They consented to meet me in council, and I then proposed to them that if they desired peace to give me palpable evidence of their sincerity by delivering into my hands their white prisoners. I told them that I was not authorized to conclude terms of peace with them, but if they acceded to my proposition I would take what chiefs they might choose to select to the Governor of Colorado Territory, state the circumstances to him, and that I believed it would result in what it was their desire to accomplish—'peace with their white brothers.' I had reference particularly to the Arapahoe and Cheyenne tribes.

"The council was divided—undecided—and could not come to an understanding among themselves. I told them that I would march to a certain locality, distant twelve miles, and await a given time for their action in the matter. I took a strong position in the locality named, and remained three days. In the interval they brought in and turned over four white prisoners, all that was possible for them at the time being to turn over, the balance of the seven being (as they stated) with another band far to the northward.

. . . . . .

"I have the principal chiefs of the two tribes with me, and propose starting immediately to Denver, to put into effect the aforementioned proposition made by me to them.

"They agree to deliver up the balance of the prisoners as soon as it is possible to procure them, which can be done better from Denver City than from this point.

"I have the honor, Governor, to be your obedient servant,
"E. W. WYNKOOP,
"Major First Col. Cav. Com'd'g
Fort Lyon, C. T.
"His Excellency, JOHN EVANS,
"Governor of Colorado, Denver, C. T."

"FORT LYON, COLORADO TERRITORY, July 26, 1864.
"SIR:
"When I last wrote you, I was in hopes that our

Indian troubles were at an end. Colonel Chivington has just arrived from Larned and gives a sad account of affairs at that post. They have killed some ten men from a train, and run off all the stock from the post.

"As near as they can learn, all the tribes were engaged in it. The colonel will give you the particulars. There is no dependence to be put in any of them. I have done everything in my power to keep the peace; I now think a little powder and lead is the best food for them.

"Respectfully, your obedient servant,
"S. G. COLLEY,
United States Indian Agent.
"Hon. JOHN EVANS,
"Governor and Superintendent Indian Affairs."

The following statement by Robert North was made to me:

"November 10, 1863.
"Having recovered an Arapahoe prisoner (a squaw) from the Utes, I obtained the confidence of the Indians completely. I have lived with them from a boy and my wife is an Arapahoe.

"In honor of my exploit in recovering the prisoner, the Indians recently gave me a 'big medicine dance' about fifty miles below Fort Lyon, on the Arkansas River, at which the leading chiefs and warriors of several of the tribes of the plains met.

"The Comanches, Apaches, Kiowas, the northern band of Arapahoes, and all of the Cheyennes, with the Sioux, have pledged one another to go to war with the whites as soon as they can procure ammunition in the spring. I have heard them discuss the matter often, and the few of them who opposed it were forced to be quiet, and were really in danger of their lives. I saw the principal chiefs pledge to each other that they would be friendly and shake hands with the whites until they procured ammunition and guns, so as to be ready when they strike. Plundering to get means has already commenced; and the plan is to commence the war at several points in the sparse settlements early in the spring. They wanted me to join them in the war, saying that they would take a great many white women and children prisoners, and get a heap of property, blankets, etc.; but while I am connected with them by marriage, and live with them, I am yet a white man, and wish to avoid bloodshed. There are many Mexicans with the Comanche and Apache Indians, all of whom urge on the war, promising to help the Indians themselves, and that a great many more Mexicans would come up from New Mexico for the purpose in the spring."

In addition to the statement showing that all the Cheyennes were in the alliance, I desire to add the following frank admission from the Indians in the council:

"Governor Evans explained that smoking the war-pipe was a figurative term, but their conduct had been such as to show that they had an understanding with other tribes.

"Several Indians: We acknowledge that our actions have given you reason to believe this."

In addition to all this, I refer to the statement of Mrs. Ewbanks. She is one of the prisoners that Black Kettle, in the council, said they had. Instead

The Battle of Sand Creek

of *purchasing* her, they first *captured* her on the Little Blue, and then *sold* her to the Sioux.

Mrs. Martin, another rescued prisoner, was *captured* by the *Cheyennes* on Plum Creek, *west of Kearney*, with a boy nine years old. These were the prisoners of which White Antelope said, in the council, "We took two prisoners west of Kearney, and destroyed the trains." In her published statement she says the party who captured her and the boy killed eleven men and destroyed the trains and were mostly *Cheyennes*.

Thus I have proved by the Indian chiefs named in the report, by Agent Colley and Major Wynkoop, to whom they refer to sustain their assertion to the contrary, that these Indians had "been at war, and had committed acts of hostility and depredations."

In regard to their status prior to their council at Denver, the foregoing public documents which I have cited show how utterly devoid of truth or foundation is the assertion that these Indians "had been friendly to the whites, and had not been guilty of any acts of hostility or depredations."

The next paragraph of the report is as follows:

"A northern band of Cheyennes, known as the 'Dog Soldiers,' had been guilty of acts of hostility; but all the testimony goes to prove that they had no connection with Black Kettle's band, and acted in spite of his authority and influence. Black Kettle and his band denied all connection with, or responsibility for, the Dog Soldiers, and Left Hand and his band were equally friendly."

The committee and the public will be surprised to learn the fact that these Dog Soldiers, on which the committee throws the *slight* blame for acts of hostility, were really among Black Kettle's and White Antelope's own warriors, in the *"friendly"* camp to which Major Wynkoop made his expedition, and their head man, Bull Bear, was one of the prominent men of the deputation brought in to see me at Denver. By reference to the report of the council with the chiefs, to which I referred the committee, it will be observed that Black Kettle and all present based their propositions to *make peace* upon the assent of *their bands*, and that these Dog Soldiers were especially referred to.

The report continues:
"These Indians, at the suggestion of Governor Evans and Colonel Chivington, repaired to Fort Lyon and placed themselves under the protection of Major Wynkoop, etc."

The connection of my name in this is again wrong. I simply left them in the hands of the military authorities, where I found them, and my action was approved by the Indian Bureau.

The following extracts from the report of the council will prove this conclusively. I stated to the Indians:

" . . . Another reason that I am not in a condition to make a treaty is, that the war is begun, and the power to make a treaty of peace has passed from me to the great war chief."

I also said: "Again, whatever peace they may make must be with the soldiers and not with me."

And again, in reply to White Antelope's inquiry, "How can we be protected from the soldiers on the plains?" I said: "You must make that arrangement with the military chief."

The morning after this council, I addressed the

following letter to the agent of these Indians, which is published in the report of the Commissioner of Indian Affairs for 1864, page 220:

"COLORADO SUPERINTENDENCY INDIAN AFFAIRS,
DENVER, September 29, 1864.
"SIR:
"The chiefs brought in by Major Wynkoop have been heard. I have declined to make any peace with them, lest it might embarrass the military operations against the hostile Indians on the plains. The Arapahoe and Cheyenne Indians being now at war with the United States Government, must make peace with the military authorities. Of course this arrangement relieves the Indian Bureau of their care until peace is declared with them; and as these tribes are yet scattered, and all except Friday's band are at war, it is not probable that it will be done immediately. You will be particular to impress upon these chiefs the fact that my talk with them was for the purpose of ascertaining their views, and not to offer them anything whatever. They must deal with the military authorities until peace, in which case, alone, they will be in proper position to treat with the government in relation to the future.

"I have the honor to be, very respectfully, your obedient servant,
"JOHN EVANS,
"Governor Colorado Territory and
"ex-officio Superintendent of Indian Affairs.
"MAJOR S. G. COLLEY,
"United States Indian Agent, Upper Arkansas."

It will thus be seen that I had, with the approval

of the Indian Bureau, turned the adjustment of difficulties with the hostile Indians entirely over to the military authorities; that I had instructed Agent Colley, at Fort Lyon, that this would relieve the Bureau of further care of the Arapahoes and Cheyennes, until peace was made, and having had no notice of such peace, or instructions to change the arrangement, the status of these Indians was in no respect within my jurisdiction, or under my official inspection.

It may be proper for me to say further, that it will appear in evidence that I had no intimation of the direction in which the campaign against the hostile Indians was to move, or against what bands it was to be made, when I left the Territory last fall, and that I was absent from Colorado when the Sand Creek battle occurred.

The report continues:

"It is true that there seems to have been excited among the people inhabiting that region of country a hostile feeling towards the Indians. Some had committed acts of hostility towards the whites, but no effort seems to have been made by the authorities there to prevent these hostilities, other than by the commission of even worse acts."

"*Some* had committed acts of hostility towards the whites!" Hear the facts: In the fall of 1863 a general alliance of the Indians of the plains was effected with the Sioux, and in the language of Bull Bear, in the report of the council, "Their plan is to clean out all this country."

The war opened early in the spring of 1864. The people of the East, absorbed in the greater interest of the rebellion, know but little of its history. Stock was stolen, ranches destroyed, houses burned, freight trains plundered, and their contents carried away or scattered upon the plains; settlers in the frontier counties murdered, or forced to seek safety for themselves and families in blockhouses and interior towns; emigrants to our Territory were surprised in their camps, children were slain, and wives taken prisoners; our trade and travel with the States were cut off; the necessities of life were at starvation prices; the interests of the Territory were being damaged to the extent of millions; every species of atrocity and barbarity which characterizes savage warfare was committed. This is no fancy sketch, but a plain statement of facts of which the committee seem to have had no proper realization. All this history of war and blood—all this history of rapine and ruin—all this story of outrage and suffering on the part of our people—is summed up by the committee, and given to the public in one mild sentence, "*Some* had committed acts of hostility against the whites."

The committee not only ignore the general and terrible character of our Indian war, and the great sufferings of our people, but make the grave charge that "no effort seems to have been made by the authorities there to prevent all these hostilities."

Had the committee taken the trouble, as they certainly should have done before making so grave a charge, to have read the public documents of the government, examined the record and files of the Indian Bureau, of the War Department, and of this superintendency, *instead of adopting the language of some hostile and irresponsible witness, as they appear to have done,* they would have found that the most earnest and persistent efforts had been made on my part to prevent hostilities. The records show that early in the spring of 1863, United States Indian Agent Loree, of the Upper Platte Agency, reported to me in person that the Sioux under his agency, and the Arapahoes and Cheyennes, were negotiating an alliance for war on the whites. I immediately wrote an urgent appeal for authority to avert the danger, and sent Agent Loree as special messenger with the dispatch to Washington. In response authority was given, and an earnest effort was made to collect the Indians in council. The following admission, in the report of the council, explains the result:

"Governor Evans: '... Hearing last fall that they were dissatisfied, the Great Father at Washington sent me out on the plains to talk with you and make it all right. I sent messengers out to tell you that I had presents, and would make you a feast; but you sent word to me that you did not want to have anything to do with me, and to the Great Father at Washington that you could get along without him. Bull Bear wanted to come in to see me, at the head of the Republican, but his people held a council and would not let him come.'

"Black Kettle: 'That is true.'

"Governor Evans: 'I was under the necessity, after all my trouble, and all the expense I was at, of returning home without seeing them. Instead of this, your people went away and smoked the war-pipe with our enemies.'"

Notwithstanding these unsuccessful efforts, I still hoped to preserve peace.

The records of these offices also show that, in the autumn of 1863, I was reliably advised from various sources that nearly all the Indians of the plains had

The Battle of Sand Creek 139

formed an alliance for the purpose of going to war in the spring, and I immediately commenced my efforts to avert the imminent danger. From that time forward, by letter, by telegram, and personal representation to the Commissioner of Indian Affairs, the Secretary of War, the commanders of the department and district; by traveling for weeks in the wilderness of the plains; by distribution of annuities and presents; by sending notice to the Indians to leave the hostile alliance; by every means within my power, I endeavored to preserve peace and protect the interests of the people of the Territory. And in the face of all this, which the records abundantly show, the committee say: "No effort seems to have been made by the authorities there to prevent these hostilities, other than by the commission of even worse acts."

They do not point out any of these acts, unless the continuation of the paragraph is intended to do so. It proceeds:

"The hatred of the whites to the Indians would seem to have been inflamed and excited to the utmost. The bodies of persons killed at a distance—whether by Indians or not is not certain—were brought to the capital of the Territory and exposed to the public gaze, for the purpose of inflaming still more the already excited feelings of the people."

There is no mention in this of anything that was done by authority, but it is so full of misrepresentation, in apology for the Indians, and unjust reflection on a people who have a right from their birth, education, and ties of sympathy with the people they so recently left behind them, to have at least a just consideration. The bodies referred to were those of the Hungate family, who were brutally murdered by the Indians, within twenty-five miles of Denver. No one here ever doubted that the Indians did it, and it was admitted by the Indians in the council. This was early in the summer, and before the notice sent in June to the friendly Indians. Their mangled bodies were brought to Denver for decent burial. Many of our people went to see them, as any people would have done. It did produce excitement and consternation, and where are the people who could have witnessed it without emotion? Would the committee have the people shut their eyes to such scenes at their very doors?

The next sentence, equally unjust and unfair, refers to my proclamation, issued two months after this occurrence, and four months before the "attack" they were investigating, and having no connection with it or with the troops engaged in it. It is as follows:

"The cupidity was appealed to, for the Governor, in a proclamation, calls upon all, either individually, or in such parties as they may organize, to kill and destroy as enemies of the country, wherever they may be found, all such hostile Indians; authorizing them to hold, to their own use and benefit, all the property of said hostile Indians they may capture. What Indians he would ever term friendly, it is impossible to tell."

I offer the following statement of the circumstances under which this proclamation was issued by the Hon. D. A. Chever. It is as follows:

"EXECUTIVE DEPARTMENT, COLORADO TERRITORY,
August 21, 1865.

"I, David A. Chever, Clerk in the office of the Governor of the territory of Colorado, do solemnly

The Battle of Sand Creek   141

swear that the people of said territory, from the Purgatoire to the Cache la Poudre rivers, a distance of over two hundred miles, and for a like distance along the Platte river, being the whole of our settlements on the plains, were thrown into the greatest alarm and consternation by numerous and almost simultaneous attacks and depredations by hostile Indians early last summer; that they left their unreaped crops, and collecting into communities built blockhouses and stockades for protection at central points throughout the long line of settlements; that those living in the vicinity of Denver City fled to it, and that the people of said city were in great fear of sharing the fate of New Ulm, Minnesota; that the threatened loss of crops, and the interruption of communication with the states by the combined hostilities, threatened the very existence of the whole people; that this feeling of danger was universal; that a flood of petitions and deputations poured into this office, from the people of all parts of the territory, praying for protection, and for arms and authority to protect themselves; that the defects of the militia law and the want of means to provide for defense was proved by the failure of this department, after the utmost endeavors, to secure an effective organization under it; that reliable reports of the presence of a large body of hostile warriors at no great distance east of this place were received, which reports were afterwards proved to be true, by the statement of Elbridge Gerry (page 232, Report of Commissioner of Indian Affairs for 1864); that repeated and urgent applications to the War Department for protection and authority to raise troops for the purpose had failed; that urgent applications to department and district commanders had failed to bring any prospect of relief, and that in the midst of this terrible consternation and apparently defenseless condition, it had been announced to this office, from district headquarters, that all the Colorado troops in the service of the United States had been peremptorily ordered away, and nearly all of them had marched to the Arkansas River, to be in position to repel the threatened invasion of the rebels into Kansas and Missouri; that reliable reports of depredations and murders by the Indians, from all parts of our extended lines of exposed settlements, became daily more numerous, until the simultaneous attacks on trains along the overland stage line were reported by telegraph, on the 8th of August, described in the letter of George K. Otis, superintendent of overland stage line, published on page 254 of Report of Commissioner of Indian Affairs for 1864. Under these circumstances, on the 11th of August, the Governor issued his proclamation to the people, calling upon them to defend their homes and families from the savage foe; that it prevented anarchy; that several militia companies immediately organized under it, and aided in inspiring confidence; that under its authority no act of impropriety has been reported, and I do not believe that any occurred; that it had no reference to or connection with the third regiment of one-hundred-days men that was subsequently raised by authority of the War Department, under a different proclamation, calling for volunteers, or with any of the troops engaged in the Sand Creek Affair, and that the reference to it in such connection in the report of the Committee on the Conduct of the War is a perversion of the history and facts in the case.

"DAVID A. CHEVER."

"Territory of Colorado, Arapahoe County, City of Denver, SS.: Subscribed and sworn to before me this 21st day of August, A.D. 1865. ELI M. ASHLEY, Notary Public."

I had appealed by telegraph, June 14th, to the War Department for authority to call the militia into the United States service, or to raise one-hundred-day troops; also had written to our delegate in Congress to see why I got no response, and had received his reply to the effect that he could learn nothing about it; had received a notice from the department commander, declining to take the responsibility of asking the militia for United States service, throwing the people entirely on the necessity of taking care of themselves.

It was under these circumstances of trial, suffering, and danger on the part of the people, and of fruitless appeal upon my part to the general government for aid, that I issued my proclamation of the 11th of August, 1864, of which the committee complains.

Without means to mount or pay militia, and failing to get government authority to raise forces, and under the withdrawal of the few troops in the Territory, could any other course be pursued?

The people were asked to fight on their own account—at their own expense—and in lieu of the protection the government failed to render. They were authorized to kill only the Indians that were murdering and robbing them in hostility, and to keep the property captured from them. How the committee would have them fight these savages, and what other disposition they would make of the property captured, the public will be curious to know. Would they fight without killing? Would they have the captured property turned over to the government, as if captured by United States troops? Would they forbid such captures? Would they restore it to the hostile tribes?

The absurdity of the committee's saying that this was an "appeal to the cupidity," is too palpable to require much comment. Would men leave high wages, mount and equip themselves at enormous expense, as some patriotically did, for the poor chance of capturing property, as a mere speculation, from the prowling bands of Indians that infested the settlements and were murdering their families? The thing is preposterous.

For this proclamation I have no apology. It had its origin and has its justification in the imperative necessities of the case. A merciless foe surrounded us. Without means to mount or pay militia, unable to secure government authority to raise forces, and our own troops ordered away, again I ask, could any other course be pursued?

Captain Tyler's and other companies organized under it, at enormous expense, left their lucrative business, high wages, and profitable employment, and served without other pay than the consciousness of having done noble and patriotic service; and no act of impropriety has ever been laid to the charge of any party acting under this proclamation. They had all been disbanded months before the "attack" was made that the committee were investigating.

The third regiment was organized under authority from the War Department, subsequently received by telegraph, and under a subsequent proclamation issued on the 13th of August, and were regularly mustered into the service of the United States about

The Battle of Sand Creek

three months before the battle the committee were investigating occurred.

Before closing this reply, it is perhaps just that I should say that when I testified before the committee, the chairman and all its members except three were absent, and I think, when the truth becomes known, this report will trace its parentage to a single member of the committee.

I have thus noticed such portions of the report as refer to myself, and shown conclusively that the committee, in every mention they have made of me, have been, to say the least, mistaken.

First: The committee, for the evident purpose of maintaining their position that these Indians had not been engaged in war, say the prisoners they held were purchased. The testimony is to the effect that they captured them.

Second: The committee say that these Indians were and always had been friendly, and had committed no acts of hostility or depredations. The public documents to which I refer show conclusively that they had been hostile, and had committed many acts of hostility and depredations.

Third: They say that I joined in sending these Indians to Fort Lyon. The published report of the Commissioner of Indian Affairs, and of the Indian council, show that I left them entirely in the hands of the military authorities.

Fourth: They say nothing seems to have been done by the authorities to prevent hostilities. The public documents and files of the Indian Bureau, and of my superintendency, show constant and unremitting diligence and effort on my part to prevent hostilities and protect the people.

Fifth: They say that I prevaricated for the purpose of avoiding the admission that these Indians "were and had been actuated by the most friendly feelings towards the whites." Public documents cited show conclusively that the admission they desired me to make was false, and that my statement, instead of being a prevarication, was true, although not in accordance with the preconceived and mistaken opinions of the committee. . . .

This report, so full of mistakes which ordinary investigation would have avoided; so full of slander, which ordinary care of the character of men would have prevented, is to be regretted, for the reason that it throws doubt upon the reliability of all reports which have emanated from the same source, during the last four years of war.

I am confident that the public will see, from the facts herein set forth, the great injustice done me; and I am further confident that the committee, when they know these and other facts I shall lay before them, will also see this injustice, and, as far as possible, repair it.

Very respectfully, your obedient servant,
JOHN EVANS, Governor of the Territory of Colorado, and ex-officio Superintendent of Indian Affairs.

CHAPTER VI

A DEFENSE OF THE BATTLE OF SAND CREEK
(*Continued*)

IF anything in addition to Governor Evans's statement were needed to prove the hostility of the Indians attacked at Sand Creek, it will be found in the admission of the Indians themselves at the council held by Governor Evans with the Cheyenne and Arapahoe chiefs in Denver about sixty days prior to the battle. At this council, there were present Black Kettle, leading chief of the Cheyennes, White Antelope, chief of the central band of the Cheyennes, Bull Bear, leader of the Cheyenne Dog Soldiers, Neva, sub-chief of the Arapahoes, and several other minor chiefs of that tribe. These chiefs admitted that their people had been, and were still committing depredations, as the following extract from the report of the council, taken down at the time, conclusively shows:

Gov. Evans: Who committed the murder of the Hungate family on Running Creek?

NEVA:	The Arapahoes, a party of the northern band who were passing north. It was the Medicine Man, or Roman Nose, and three others. I am satisfied from the time he left a certain camp for the north, that it was this party of four persons.
AGT. WHITLEY:	That cannot be true.
GOV. EVANS:	Where is Roman Nose?
NEVA:	You ought to know better than me, you have been nearer to him.
GOV. EVANS:	Who killed the man and boy at the head of Cherry Creek?
NEVA:	(After consultation) Kiowas and Comanches.
GOV. EVANS:	Who stole the horses and mules from Jimmy's Camp twenty-seven days ago?
NEVA:	*Fourteen Cheyennes and Arapahoes together.*
GOV. EVANS:	What were their names?
NEVA:	Powder Face and Whirlwind, *who are now in our camp, were the leaders.*
COL. SHOUP:	I counted twenty Indians on that occasion.
GOV. EVANS:	Who stole Charlie Autobee's horses?
NEVA:	Raven's son.
GOV. EVANS:	I suppose you acknowledge the depredations on the Little Blue, as you have the prisoners then taken in your possession?

The Battle of Sand Creek 149

WHITE ANTELOPE: We [the Cheyennes] took two prisoners west of Ft. Kearney and destroyed the trains.

It will be seen from the foregoing, that these Indians, although pretending to be friendly, had to admit that their people stole the horses from the soldiers at Jimmy's Camp, near Colorado City, an account of which I have already given, and that the Indians who did it were in their camp at Sand Creek at the time the council was being held. They lied concerning the man and boy killed at the head of Cherry Creek, for they knew that the Kiowas and Comanches never came this far north, and that the murders were committed by their own people. Neva's admission that Raven's son stole Charlie Autobee's horses proved the hostility of the Arapahoes, as Raven was the head chief of that tribe.

At the time the council was being held, General S. R. Curtis, commanding the military district, sent the following telegram to Colonel Chivington, evidently fearing that peace would be made prematurely.

FT. LEAVENWORTH,
September 28th, 1864.

TO COLONEL CHIVINGTON:
I shall require the bad Indians delivered up; re-

storation of equal numbers of stock; also hostages to secure. I want no peace till the Indians suffer more. Left Hand is said to be a good chief of the Arapahoes but Big Mouth is a rascal. I fear the Agent of the Indian Department will be ready to make presents too soon. It is better to chastise before giving anything but a little tobacco to talk over. No peace must be made without my direction.

S. R. Curtis, Major-General.

On November 2, 1864, Major Wynkoop was relieved of the command at Fort Lyon, and Major Anthony, of the First Regiment of Colorado Cavalry, was appointed his successor. The reason given for the removal of Major Wynkoop was that he was inclined to temporize with the hostile Indians, contrary to the orders of his superior officers.

In a report made by Major Anthony to his superior officer from Fort Lyon, under date of November 6, 1864, he says:

Nine Cheyenne Indians to-day sent in wishing to see me. They state that six hundred of that tribe are now thirty-five miles north of here coming toward the post, and two thousand about seventy-five miles away waiting for better weather to enable them to come in.

I shall not permit them to come in even as prisoners, for the reason that if I do, I shall have to subsist them upon a prisoner's rations. I shall, however, de-

The Battle of Sand Creek 151

mand their arms, all stolen stock, and the perpetrators of all depredations. I am of the opinion that they will not accept this proposition, but that they will return to the Smoky Hill.

They pretend that they want peace, and I think they do now, as they cannot fight during the winter, except where a small band of them can fight an unprotected train or frontier settlement. I do not think it is policy to make peace with them until all perpetrators of depredations are surrendered up to be dealt with as we may propose.

This report was dated only twenty-three days before the battle of Sand Creek occurred. The Indians Major Anthony mentions as camped thirty-five miles away were those that were attacked by Colonel Chivington. That they were not, and had not been under Major Anthony's protection, and that he considered them hostile, is clearly shown by the above report as well as by the testimony given by him March 14, 1865, in an investigation of the battle of Sand Creek made by the Joint Committee on the Conduct of the War, as is shown by the following extracts:

"You say you held a conference with the Indians. State what occurred?"

"At the time I took command of the post, there was a band of Arapahoe Indians encamped about a mile from the post, numbering, in men, women, and children, 652. They were visiting the post almost every day. I met them and had a talk with them. Among them was Left Hand, who was a chief among the Arapahoes. He with his band was with the party at the time. I talked with them and they proposed to do whatever I said; whatever I said for them to do, they would do. I told them that I could not feed them; that I could not give them anything to eat; that there were positive orders forbidding that; that I could not permit them to come within the limits of the post. At the same time they might remain where they were and I would treat them as prisoners of war if they remained; that they would have to surrender to me all their arms, and turn over to me all stolen property they had taken from the government or citizens. These terms they accepted. They turned over to me some twenty head of stock, mules and horses, and a few arms, but not a quarter of the arms that report stated they had in their possession. The arms they turned over to me were almost useless. I fed them for some ten days. At the end of that time I told them that I could not feed them any more; that they better go out to the buffalo country where they could kill game to subsist upon. I returned their arms to them and they left the post. But before leaving they sent word out to the Cheyennes that I was not very friendly towards them."

"How do you know that?"

"Through several of their chiefs: Neva, an Arapahoe chief, Left Hand, of the Arapahoes; then Black Kettle and War Bonnet, of the Cheyennes."

"What property did they turn over?"

"Fourteen head of mules and six head of horses."

"Was it property purporting to have been stolen by them?"

The Battle of Sand Creek

"Yes, sir."

"From whom?"

"They did not say, yet some of it was recognized; some of it was branded 'U. S.' Some was recognized as being stock that belonged to citizens. It was generally understood afterwards—I did not know it at the time—that the son of the head chief of the Arapahoes, Little Raven, and I think another, had attacked a small government train and killed one man. . . ."

"Who was the chief of that band?"

"Little Raven was the chief of those I held as prisoners. . . .

"A delegation of the Cheyennes, numbering, I suppose, fifty or sixty men, came in just before the Arapahoes left the post. I met them outside the post and talked with them. They said they wanted to make peace; that they had no desire to fight against us any longer. I told them that I had no authority from department headquarters to make peace with them; that I could not permit them to visit the post and come within the lines; that when they had been permitted to do so at Fort Larned, while the squaws and children of the different tribes that visited the post were dancing in front of the officers' quarters and on the parade ground, the Indians had made an attack on the post, fired on the guard, and run off the stock, and I was afraid the same thing might occur at Fort Lyon. I would not permit them to visit the post at all. I told them I could make no offers of peace to them until I heard from district headquarters. I told them, however, that they might go out and camp on Sand Creek, and remain there if they chose to do so; but they should not camp in the vicinity of the post; that if I had authority to go out and make peace with them, I would go out and let them know of it.

"In the meantime I was writing to district headquarters constantly, stating to them that there was a band of Indians within forty miles of the post—a small band—while a very large band was about 100 miles from the post. That I was strong enough with the force I had with me to fight the Indians on Sand Creek, but not strong enough to fight the main band. That I should try to keep the Indians quiet until such time as I received reinforcements; and that as soon as reinforcements did arrive we should go further and find the main party.

"But before the reinforcements came from district headquarters, Colonel Chivington came to Fort Lyon with his command, and I joined him and went out on that expedition to Sand Creek. I never made any offer to the Indians. It was the understanding that I was not in favor of peace with them. They so understood me, I suppose; at least I intended they should. In fact, I often heard of it through their interpreters that they did not suppose we were friendly towards them. . . .

"This is the way in which we had been situated out there. I have been in command of a body of troops at Fort Larned or Fort Lyon for upwards of two years. About two years ago in September the Indians were professing to be perfectly friendly. These were the Cheyennes, the Comanches, the Apaches, the Arapahoes, the Kiowas, encamped at different points on the Arkansas River between Fort Larned and Fort Lyon. Trains were going up to Fort Lyon frequently and scarcely a train came in but had some complaint

The Battle of Sand Creek

to make about the Indians. I recollect that one particular day three trains came in to the post and reported to me that the Indians had robbed them of their provisions. We at the post had to issue provisions to them constantly. Trains that were carrying government freight to New Mexico would stop there and get their supplies replenished on account of the Indians having taken theirs on the road.

"At one time I took two pieces of artillery and 125 men, and went down to meet the Indians. As soon as I got there they were apparently friendly. A Kiowa chief perhaps would say to me that his men were perfectly friendly, and felt all right towards the whites, but the Arapahoes were very bad Indians. Go to the Arapahoe camp, and they would perhaps charge everything upon the Comanches; while the Comanches would charge it upon the Cheyennes; yet each band there was professing friendship towards us. . . .

"When the Indians took their prisoners (in fact, however, they generally took no prisoners) near Simmering Spring, they killed ten men. I was told by Captain Davis, of the California volunteers, that the Indians cut off the heads of the men after they had scalped them, and piled them in a pile on the ground, and danced around them, and kicked their bodies around over the ground, etc. It is the general impression of the people of that country that the only way to fight Indians is to fight them as they fight us; if they scalp and mutilate the bodies we must do the same.

"I recollect one occasion, when I had a fight on Pawnee fork with the Indians there, I had fifty-nine men with me, and the Indians numbered several hundred. I was retreating and they had followed me about five miles. I had eleven men of my party shot at that time. I had with my party then a few Delaware Indians, and one Captain Fall Leaf, of the Delaware tribe, had his horse shot; we had to stop every few minutes, dismount, and fire upon the Indians to keep them off. They formed a circle right around us. Finally we shot down one Indian very close to us. I saw Fall Leaf make a movement as though he wanted to scalp the Indian. I asked him if he wanted that Indian's scalp and he said he did. We kept up a fire to keep the Indians off, while he went down and took off his scalp, and gave his Delaware war-whoop. That seemed to strike more terror into those Indians than anything else we had done that day. And I do think if it had not been for that one thing, we should have lost a great many more of my men. I think it struck terror to them so that they kept away from us."

"Did the troops mutilate the Indians killed at Sand Creek?"

"*They did in some instances that I know of, but I saw nothing to the extent I have since heard stated.*"

"Did you not feel that you were bound in good faith not to attack those Indians after they had surrendered to you and after they had taken up a position which you yourself had indicated?"

"I did not consider that they had surrendered to me; I never would consent that they should surrender to me. My instructions were such that I felt in duty bound to fight them wherever I found them; provided I considered it good policy to do so. I did not consider it good policy to attack this party of Indians

The Battle of Sand Creek 157

on Sand Creek unless I was strong enough to go on and fight the main band at the Smoke Hills, some seventy miles further. If I had had that force, I should have gone out and fought this band on Sand Creek. . . ."

"You think the attack made upon those Indians, in addition to the other characteristics which it possesses, was impolitic?"

"I do, very much so. I think it was the occasion of what has occurred on the Platte since that time. I have so stated in my report to the headquarters of the district and of the department. I stated before Colonel Chivington arrived there that the Indians were encamped at this point; that I had a force with me sufficiently strong to go out and fight them; but that I did not think it policy to do so, for I was not strong enough to fight the main band. If I fought this band, the main band would immediately strike the settlements. But so soon as the party should be strong enough to fight the main band, I should be in favor of making the war general against the Indians. I stated to them also that I did not believe we could fight one band without fighting them all; that in case we fought one party of Indians and whipped them, those that escaped would go into another band that was apparently friendly and that band would secrete those who had been committing depredations before. As it was with Little Raven's band; his own sons attacked a train a short distance above Fort Lyon, killed one soldier, took a government wagon and mules, some horses, and took some women prisoners. One woman they afterwards outraged and she hung herself; the other one, I think, they still hold. Some of the Indians have married her, as they call it, and she is still in their camp, as I have understood; not now in the camp of those who took her prisoner, but she has been sold to the Sioux and Cheyennes. The instructions we constantly received from the headquarters both of the district and the department, were that we should show as little mercy to the Indians as possible. . . ."

In another part of his testimony, Major Anthony said referring to the Arapahoes, "I considered them differently from the Cheyennes," and when asked if they were with the Cheyennes at Sand Creek, replied, "I understood, afterwards, that some six or eight or ten lodges of the Arapahoes were there."

Major S. G. Colley, the Indian agent, said in his testimony, "Left Hand's band had gone out to Sand Creek," and when asked how many were in Left Hand's band, replied, "About eight lodges of about five to the lodge."

If there were no other evidence, the following telegrams from General Curtis, Commander of the Department of Missouri, are in themselves sufficient proofs of the hostility of both Cheyennes and Arapahoes:

FT. LEAVENWORTH, April 8th, 1864.
TO COLONEL CHIVINGTON:
I hear that Indians have committed depredations

The Battle of Sand Creek 159

on or near Platte River. Do not let district lines prevent pursuing and punishing them.

S. R. CURTIS, Major-General.

FT. LEAVENWORTH, May 30th, 1864.
To COLONEL CHIVINGTON:
Some four hundred Cheyennes attacked Lieut. Clayton on Smoky Hill. After several hours fight the Indians fled, leaving twenty-eight killed. Our loss four killed and three wounded. Look out for Cheyennes everywhere. Especially instruct troops in upper Arkansas.

S. R. CURTIS, Major-General.

FT. LEAVENWORTH, October 7, 1864.
MAJOR-GENERAL HALLECK, Chief of Staff:
General Blunt came upon a party of Arapahoes and other hostile Indians supposed to be four thousand, with fifteen hundred warriors, on the twenty-fifth ultimo. This was about one hundred miles west of Larned on Pawnee fork. The Indians overpowered the advance, but the main force coming up routed and pursued them. Ninety-one dead Indians were left and we lost two killed and seven wounded. General Blunt's force was less than five hundred. He pursued for several days.

S. R. CURTIS, Major-General.

The place where this battle occurred was about one hundred and thirty miles east of the Sand Creek battle-ground, and probably some of the same Indians were in both encounters.

The telegrams I have quoted indicate that

General Curtis was fully alive to the situation. Evidently he believed the Cheyennes and Arapahoes were hostile and was not in favor of making peace with them until they had been punished.

On account of his limited force, Colonel Chivington could do little more than protect the lines of travel; consequently, all that summer and fall the frontier settlers were compelled to take care of themselves. And it was not until after the Third Colorado had been organized and equipped that he was able to strike a decisive blow. In his deposition presented at the investigation by the Joint Committee on the Conduct of the War, among other things, Colonel Chivington has the following to say concerning the battle of Sand Creek and the conditions leading up to it.

"On the 29th day of November, 1864, the troops under my command attacked a camp of Cheyenne and Arapahoe Indians at a place known as Big Bend of Sandy, about forty miles north of Fort Lyon, Colorado Territory. There were in my command at that time about (500) five hundred men of the Third Regiment Colorado cavalry, under the immediate command of Colonel George L. Shoup, of said Third Regiment, and about (250) two hundred and fifty men of the First Colorado cavalry; Major Scott J. Anthony commanded one battalion of said First regiment, and Lieutenant Luther Wilson commanded another battalion of said First regiment.

The Third regiment was armed with rifled muskets, and Star's and Sharp's carbines. A few of the men of that regiment had revolvers. The men of the First regiment were armed with Star's and Sharp's carbines, and revolvers. The men of the Third regiment were poorly equipped; the supply of blankets, boots, hats, and caps was deficient. The men of the First regiment were well equipped; all of these troops were mounted. 1 had four 12-pound mountain howitzers, manned by detachments from cavalry companies; they did not belong to any battery company.

"From the best and most reliable information I could obtain, there were in the Indian camp, at the time of the attack, about eleven or twelve hundred Indians; of these about seven hundred were warriors and the remainder were women and children. I am not aware that there were any old men among them. *There was an unusual number of males among them, for the reason that the war chiefs of both nations were assembled there, evidently for some special purpose.* . . ."

"What number did you lose in killed, and what number in wounded and what number in missing?"

"There were seven men killed, forty-seven wounded, and one was missing.

"From the best information I could obtain, I judge that there were five or six hundred Indians killed; I cannot state positively the number killed, nor can I state positively the number of women and children killed. Officers who passed over the field, by my orders, report that they saw but few women and children dead, no more than would certainly fall in an attack upon a camp in which they were. I myself passed over some portions of the field after the fight, and *I saw but one woman who had been killed, and one who had hanged herself; I saw no dead children. From all I could learn, I arrived at the conclusion that but few women or children had been slain. I am of the opinion that when the attack was made on the Indian camp the greater number of squaws and children made their escape, while the warriors remained to fight my troops.*

"I do not know that any Indians were wounded that were not killed; if there were any wounded, I do not think they could have been made prisoners without endangering the lives of the soldiers; Indians usually fight as long as they have strength to resist. Eight Indians fell into the hands of the troops alive, to my knowledge; these with one exception were sent to Fort Lyon and properly cared for. . . .

"My reason for making the attack on the Indian camp was that I believed the Indians in the camp were hostile to the whites. That they were of the same tribes with those who had murdered many persons and destroyed much valuable property on the Platte and Arkansas rivers during the previous spring, summer, and fall was beyond a doubt. When a tribe of Indians is at war with the whites, it is impossible to determine what party or band of the tribe or the name of the Indian or Indians belonging to the tribe so at war, are guilty of the acts of hostility. The most that can be ascertained is that Indians of the tribe have performed the acts. During the spring, summer, and fall of the year 1864, the Arapahoe and Cheyenne Indians, in some instances assisted or led on by Sioux, Kiowas, Comanches, and Apaches, had committed many acts of hostility in the country lying between the Little Blue and the Rocky Mountains and the Platte and Arkansas rivers. They had

The Battle of Sand Creek

murdered many of the whites and taken others prisoners, and had destroyed valuable property, probably amounting to $200,000 or $300,000. Their rendezvous was on the headwaters of the Republican, probably one hundred miles from where the Indian camp was located. I had every reason to believe that these Indians were either directly or indirectly concerned in the outrages that had been committed upon the whites. I had no means of ascertaining what were the names of the Indians who had committed these outrages other than the declarations of the Indians themselves; and the character of Indians in the western country for truth and veracity, like their respect for the chastity of women who may become prisoners in their hands, is not of that order which is calculated to inspire confidence in what they may say. In this view I was supported by Major Anthony, 1st Colorado Cavalry, commanding at Fort Lyon, and Samuel G. Colley, United States Indian Agent, who, as they had been in communication with these Indians, were more competent to judge of their disposition toward the whites than myself. Previous to the battle they expressed to me the opinion that the Indians should be punished. We found in the camp the scalps of nineteen white persons. One of the surgeons informed me that one of these scalps had been taken from the victim's head not more than four days previously. I can furnish a child captured at camp ornamented with six white women's scalps. These scalps must have been taken by these Indians or furnished to them for their gratification and amusement by some of their brethren, who, like themselves, were in amity with the whites.

"I had no reason to believe that Black Kettle and the Indians with him were in good faith at peace with the whites. The day before the attack Major Scott J. Anthony, 1st Colorado Cavalry, then commander at Fort Lyon, told me that these Indians were hostile; that he had ordered his sentinels to fire on them if they attempted to come into the post, and that the sentinels had fired on them; that he was apprehensive of an attack from these Indians and had taken every precaution to prevent a surprise. Major Samuel G. Colley, United States Indian Agent for these Indians, told me on the same day that he had done everything in his power to make them behave themselves, and that for the last six months he could do nothing with them; that nothing but a sound whipping would bring a lasting peace with them. These statements were made to me in the presence of the officers of my staff whose statements can be obtained to corroborate the foregoing. . . .

"Since August, 1863, I had been in possession of the most conclusive evidence of the alliance, for the purposes of hostility against the whites, of the Sioux, Cheyennes, Arapahoes, Comanche, Kiowa and Apache Indians.

"Their plan was to interrupt, or, if possible, entirely prevent all travel on the routes along the Arkansas and Platte rivers, from the states to the Rocky Mountains, and thereby depopulate this country. . . .

"With very few troops at my command, I could do little to protect the settlers, except to collect the latest intelligence from the Indians' country, communicate it to General Curtis, commanding department of Missouri, and warn the settlers of the relations

The Battle of Sand Creek 165

existing between the Indians and the whites, and the probability of trouble, all of which I did. . . .

"Commanding only a district with very few troops under my control, with hundreds of miles between my headquarters and the rendezvous of the Indians, with a large portion of the Santa Fe and Platte routes, besides the sparsely settled and distant settlements of this Territory to protect, I could not do anything till the 3rd regiment was organized and equipped, when I determined to strike a blow against this savage and determined foe. When I reached Fort Lyon, after passing over from three to five feet of snow, and greatly suffering from the intensity of the cold, the thermometer ranging from 28 to 30 degrees below zero, I questioned Major Anthony in regard to the whereabouts of hostile Indians. He said there was a camp of Cheyennes and Arapahoes about fifty miles distant; that he would have attacked before, but did not consider his force sufficient; that these Indians had threatened to attack the post, etc., and ought to be whipped, all of which was concurred in by Major Colley, Indian agent for the district of the Arkansas, which information with the positive orders of Major-General Curtis, commanding the department, to punish these Indians, decided my course, and resulted in the battle of Sand Creek, which has created such a sensation in Congress through the lying reports of interested and malicious parties.

"On my arrival at Fort Lyon, in all my conversations with Major Anthony, commanding the post, and Major Colley, Indian Agent, I heard nothing of this recent statement that the Indians were under the protection of the government, etc., but Major Anthony repeatedly stated to me that he had at different times fired upon these Indians, and that they were hostile, and, during my stay at Fort Lyon, urged the necessity of my immediately attacking the Indians before they could learn of the number of troops at Fort Lyon, and so desirous was Major Colley, Indian agent, that I should find and also attack the Arapahoes, that he sent a messenger after the fight at Sand Creek nearly forty miles to inform me where I could find the Arapahoes and Kiowas; yet, strange to say, I have learned recently that these men, Anthony and Colley, are the most bitter in their denunciations of the attack upon the Indians at Sand Creek. Therefore, I would, in conclusion, most respectfully demand, as an act of justice to myself and the brave men whom I have had the honor to command in one of the hardest campaigns ever made in this country, whether against white men or red, that we be allowed the right guaranteed to every American citizen, of introducing evidence in our behalf to sustain us in what we believe to have been an act of duty to ourselves and to civilization."

Colonel George L. Shoup, in a deposition presented to the military commission investigating the battle of Sand Creek, among other things, says:

On or about the 12th of November, 1864, I left Denver for Fort Lyon, with Companies C, D, and F of my regiment and Company H of the First Colorado Cavalry, and on or about the 18th of November joined Major Sayre at Boonville with that portion of the regiment which had been left at Bijou Basin

The Battle of Sand Creek

(he having been ordered to precede me), consisting of Companies A, B, and E, and I and M. On or about the 20th Captain Baxter joined the command with Company G, and the day following Colonel John M. Chivington, commander of the district of Colorado, arrived and assumed command of the column, I still commanding my regiment. On or about the 22d the column, consisting of my regiment and a battalion of the first, marched from Boonville towards Fort Lyon and reached Fort Lyon on the 28th, and went into camp. On the evening of the 28th I received orders from the colonel commanding to prepare three days' cooked rations, and be ready to march at eight o'clock the same evening. At eight o'clock the column marched in the following order: the first regiment on the right, my regiment on the left. I had under my immediate command between five hundred and fifty and six hundred men mounted. My transportation was left at Fort Lyon. The column marched all night in a northerly direction. About daylight the next morning came in sight of an Indian village. Colonel Chivington and myself being about three-fourths of a mile in advance of the column, it was determined to make an immediate attack. Lieutenant Wilson, commanding a battalion of the first, was ordered to cut off the ponies of the Indians at the northeast of the village. By order of Colonel Chivington, I was ordered to send men to the southwest of the village, to cut off the ponies in that direction, and then to immediately engage the Indians.

"Did Colonel Chivington make any remarks to the troops, in your hearing?"

"He did not."

"Did you approach the camp of the Indians

in line of battle with your men mounted, or dismounted?"

"Kept my men in columns of fours till I arrived at the village, when I formed them in line of battle, and to the left of a battalion of the first, commanded by Lieutenant Wilson, my men mounted."

"At what distance was your command from the village when you commenced fire upon it?"

"I did not allow my men to fire when I formed my first line; the battalion on my right was firing. I wheeled my men into column of fours and marched to the rear of the battalion on my right, to the right of that battalion, to obtain a better position. I marched up Sand Creek some distance, following the Indians who were retreating up the creek. When opposite the main body of Indians, wheeled my men into line, dismounted, and opened fire."

"Did you know what band of Indians it was at the time of the attack?"

"I heard while at Fort Lyon that Left Hand, of the Arapahoes, and Black Kettle, of the Cheyennes, were at the village."

"Did you, at any time prior to the attack, hear Colonel Chivington say that he was going to attack Black Kettle's band?"

"I did not."

"How long did the fight last?"

"The fighting did not entirely cease until about three o'clock in the afternoon."

"Did you camp with your regiment near the battle-ground?"

"We camped on ground occupied by the Indians before the battle."

"What was done with the Indians and other property?"

"The lodges were burned. The ponies, numbering, as I was told, five hundred and four, were placed in charge of the provost marshal. A few remained in the hands of the troops."

"What were the casualties of your regiment?"

"Ten killed, one missing, about forty wounded."

"In your opinion how many Indians were killed?"

"From my own observation I should say about three hundred."

"Were they men, or women and children?"

"Some of each."

"Did you witness any scalping or other mutilation of the dead by your command?"

"I saw one or two men who were in the act of scalping, but I am not positive."

. . . .

"Were you present in council with some Indian chiefs in Denver, some time last summer or fall?"

"I was."

"Who were present—whites and Indians?"

"Governor Evans, Colonel Chivington, Captain S. M. Robbins, Major Wynkoop, Major Whiteley, Amos Steck, J. Bright Smith, Nelson Sargent, Captain John Wanless, Black Kettle, White Antelope, and five or six other Indians, and John Smith and Sam Ashcroft, interpreters."

"Did the Indians express a desire for peace with the whites?"

"Yes."

"Upon what terms did they desire peace?"

"That they have protection and supplies while the war was carried on against hostile Indians."

"Was peace guaranteed to them on any terms?"

"They were told by Colonel Chivington that if they would come in and surrender themselves, he would then tell them what to do."

"What did the governor tell them?"

"That as they had violated all treaties they would have to treat with the military authorities, to whom he had given up all the authority."

"Did Colonel Chivington tell them that he would guarantee them peace only on condition that they would come into the post and lay down their arms?"

"Colonel Chivington did not guarantee them peace upon any terms, but if they would come into the post, surrender themselves, and lay down their arms, he would tell them what to do."

"Did the Indians say that they would do so?"

"They said that they would go back to their people, tell them and advise them to do so."

. . . .

"Did you have any conversation with Major Colley, Indian agent for the Arapahoes and Cheyennes of the Upper Arkansas, respecting the disposition of the Indians and the policy that ought to be pursued towards them? If so, state what he said."

"I had an interview with Major Colley, on the evening of the 28th of November, in which he stated to me that these Indians had violated their treaty; that there were a few Indians that he would not like to see punished, but as long as they affiliated with the hostile Indians we could not discriminate; that no treaty could be made that would be lasting till they were all severely chastised; he also told me where these Indians were camped."

"State what you heard Major Scott J. Anthony

say in reference to these Indians on the 28th of November last."

"He said he would have fought these Indians before if he had had a force strong enough to do so, and left a sufficient garrison at Fort Lyon, he being at the time in command of Fort Lyon."

The Hon. S. H. Elbert, Acting Governor of Colorado, in a message to the Legislature, a few months after the affair, reflects the general attitude of the people toward the battle, and those participating in it. The following is an extract from it:

The before unbroken peace of our Territory has been disturbed since the last spring, by an Indian war. Allied and hostile tribes have attacked our frontier settlements, driven in our settlers, destroyed their homes, attacked, burned, and plundered our freight and emigrant trains, and thus suspended agricultural pursuits in portions of our country, and interrupted our trade and commerce with the States. This has for the time seriously retarded the prosperity of our Territory.

At the commencement of the war the General Government, taxed to the utmost in subduing the rebellion, was unable to help us, and it became necessary to look to our own citizens for protection. They everywhere responded with patriotism and alacrity. Militia companies were organized in the frontier counties and secured local protection. Much credit is due to Captain Tyler's company of militia for the important service they rendered in opening and protecting our line of communication with the States.

In response to the call of the governor for a regiment of cavalry for one hundred day service, over a thousand of our citizens—the large majority of them leaving lucrative employment—rapidly volunteered, and in that short time, despite the greatest difficulties in securing proper equipments, organized, armed, made a long and severe campaign amid the snows and storms of winter, and visited upon these merciless murderers of the plains a chastisement smiting and *deserved*. The gratitude of the country is due to the men who thus sacrificed so largely their personal interests for the public good, and rendered such important service to the Territory; and their work, if it can be followed up with a vigorous winter campaign, would result in a permanent peace.

The necessity of such a campaign, and the imperative demand for immediate and complete protection for our line of communication with the States has been, and is now being, earnestly urged on the Government at Washington, and with a prospect of success. These efforts should be seconded by your honorable body with whatever influence there may be in resolution or memorial, setting forth the facts and necessities of our situation.

The testimony of Governor Evans, Major Anthony, Colonel Chivington, Colonel Shoup, and Acting Governor Elbert covers every phase of the matter in controversy. Governor Evans's statement proves beyond question that the Cheyennes and Arapahoes were viciously hostile during the entire summer preceding the battle of Sand Creek,

The Battle of Sand Creek 173

and this was admitted by Black Kettle in his letter to Major Colley, the Indian agent, and by the other chiefs in the council at Denver. Governor Evans also makes it plain that he refused to consider the question of making peace, and turned the Indians over to the military. The telegram of General Curtis, commander of the Military Department, sent at the time the council was being held, says, "No peace must be made without my direction." And peace had not been made when the battle was fought. Major Anthony, commander of the military post of Fort Lyon, near the Cheyenne and Arapahoe Indian agency, says that the Indians attacked were hostile and not under his protection, and that he would have punished them had his force been strong enough to fight also the large band on the Smoky Hill River. Colonel Chivington's testimony confirms the statement of Governor Evans as to the hostility of both Cheyennes and Arapahoes, and both he and Colonel Shoup say that this was corroborated by Major Anthony, and Major Colley, the Indian agent, each of whom told them, while at Fort Lyon prior to the battle, that the Indians camped on Sand Creek were hostile and should be punished. Major Anthony admits that there were Arapahoes camped near the Fort when he assumed command, and that, in compliance with his demand, they surrendered twenty head of stock, stolen from the whites, and a few worthless guns; and added that a week or two later he returned the guns, and told the Indians that he could no longer feed them and ordered them to go out on the plains, where they could kill buffalo for food; whereupon they left.

The only Arapahoes that by any stretch of the imagination could be said to have been under the protection of the military were the small part of the tribe under the control of Left Hand, a sub-chief; while there is no doubt whatever as to the hostility of the head chief Raven and his followers, who constituted a large majority of the tribe. It is generally conceded that the chief Left Hand and a few of his adherents were peaceably inclined. But, unfortunately, he and the occupants of six or eight lodges of his people, about forty persons in all, including women and children, were in the camp of the hostile Cheyennes and Arapahoes at the time the attack was made, and suffered accordingly. Left Hand knew that the Cheyennes and a very large part of his own people were at war with the whites, and of the chance he was taking in being in company with the hostiles. If it resulted disastrously, he had

The Battle of Sand Creek 175

no one but himself to blame. It was utterly impossible to discriminate between Indians in the midst of the battle. In those days, Indians seldom permitted themselves to be taken prisoners in battle, and an attempt to do so, even if the Indian was badly wounded, was a dangerous undertaking. This was the reason that no prisoners were taken at Sand Creek. Major Anthony, who was not friendly to Colonel Chivington, says that while in some instances the Indians killed at Sand Creek were mutilated, he saw nothing to the extent since stated.

Colonel Chivington's statement concerning the matter is:

Officers who passed over the field by my orders after the battle, for the purpose of ascertaining the number of Indians killed, report that they saw but few women and children dead; no more than would certainly fall in an attack upon a camp in which they were. I myself passed over some portions of the field after the fight, and saw but one woman who had been killed and one who had hanged herself. I saw no dead children.

In this connection, I wish to refer back to my own statement concerning the matter, as Colonel Chivington's observations were identical with mine.

All this shows that the charge that the battle

was merely a massacre is as untruthful as are most of the other statements made by the coterie of disgruntled army officers, Indian agents, traders, interpreters, and half-breeds. Much of the testimony given at the Congressional and military hearings was hearsay evidence of statements said to have been made by persons who claimed to have been in the battle. Possibly, some such statements may have been made by irresponsible braggarts belonging to the two regiments that formed the command, for in every regiment during the Rebellion, Eastern as well as Western, there were a few men who were no credit to their comrades, and who have since told of many fictitious happenings, or those having only the slightest basis of truth. Statements of this character may, perhaps, have been made by irresponsible members of the First and Third Colorado regiments.

It is inconceivable to any one who knew the members of the latter regiment that either its officers or enlisted men, with possibly a rare exception, would have approved of, and much less have participated in, the wanton acts of cruelty claimed to have been perpetrated. No unprejudiced person can believe a charge of such a character against Colonel Shoup, afterwards for many years an honored United States Senator from the State

The Battle of Sand Creek 177

of Idaho; or of Major Hal Sayre, one of Colorado's most respected mining engineers; or of Captain Harper Orahood, who, later, was for many years a law partner of Senator H. M. Teller; or of Captain Baxter of Pueblo, or Captain Nichols of Boulder, both afterwards members of the Legislature of Colorado and honored citizens in the community in which they lived; or in fact against any of the officers of the Third Colorado, as practically all of them were men of high standing in their respective communities.

I was on the battle-field within fifteen minutes after the fight began, and during the day, with a part of our company, I went along the south side of Sand Creek from the scene of one engagement to another, until I had covered the full length of the battle-field on that side of the creek. We then crossed over to the north side and followed up the creek as far as the engagement had extended. On our return to camp, we went over the entire length of the scene of the fighting on the north side of the creek, thus covering almost the entire battle-field, as after the first half-hour in the morning there was but little fighting except near the banks of the creek. During that time I saw much of the battle, but not once did I see any one shoot at a squaw or a child, nor did I see any one take a scalp, although it is true that scalps were taken, for as I returned to camp I saw a number of dead Indians whose scalps had been taken, and among them a few squaws. They had probably been scalped by some of the reckless persons referred to, or possibly by some of the many men in the regiment whose relatives or friends had been killed and brutally mutilated by the savages during the preceding summer. I am not apologizing for the acts of these people, but every fair-minded person must admit that there may have been extenuating circumstances connected with the offense, and no one unfamiliar with the horrors of savage warfare can appreciate the feelings of those who have suffered from their attacks. I did not see a dead or wounded child, and it is inconceivable that any were killed during the fight except accidentally. The incident of the child who wished me to take it up as I was returning to the camp indicates the sympathetic attitude of our men towards the innocent non-combatants.

I think the proof I have presented shows conclusively that every one of the charges made by the enemies of Colonel Chivington was untrue; that, on the contrary, the Indians attacked at Sand Creek were, and had been during the previous summer, viciously hostile to the whites; that they

The Battle of Sand Creek 179

were not under the protection of the military authorities at Fort Lyon, and that the battle was not a wanton massacre.

The adverse criticism of this whole affair was but one of the many acts of injustice experienced by the frontier settlers. From the formation of the Government, up to the time when the Indians were finally placed upon reservations, the frontier settlements, in addition to defending themselves from the savages, always had to contend with the sentimental feeling in favor of the Indians that prevailed in the East. The people of the East had apparently forgotten the atrocities perpetrated on their ancestors by the savages, and, resting secure in the safety of their own homes, they could not realize the privations and dangers that those who were opening up the regions of the West had to endure. And to add to the difficulties of the situation, the Indian Department was usually dominated by sentimental people who apparently never had any conception of a proper and humane method of dealing with the Indians.

The Government continued to recognize each one of the tribes as a separate nation, and entered into treaties with them, as though they had the standing of an independent and responsible power. Broken down and often corrupt men were appointed as agents to represent the Government. The salaries received by the agents were so small that no one could afford to take the position unless he intended to increase his remuneration by corrupt methods. As a part of this machinery for dealing with the Indians, disreputable white men were employed as interpreters, who, often by reason of some crime committed in the States, had for safety's sake exiled themselves among the Indians, had married squaws, and, virtually, had become Indians in habits and sympathy. The result was that when the Government made treaties with the Indians, accompanied by an issue of annuities, it frequently happened that the agent and the interpreter would apply a considerable portion of such annuities to their own use. The Indians, knowing this, would become angry and take vengeance upon the white settler.

No effort seems to have been made to study the nature and character of the Indian, nor the inherited traits that governed him in his dealings with others. The nomadic Indian of the central and western part of the United States was, in most matters, merely a child. His sole occupation from youth to old age was following the chase and fighting his enemies. Almost the sole topic of conversation in their tents and around their camp-

The Battle of Sand Creek 181

fires was the details of their hunting expeditions and of their battles; and from his earliest days, every Indian boy was taught that his one hope of glory and the making of a reputation depended upon his ability to kill other human beings. Every tribe had its hereditary enemies with whom it was in a state of continuous warfare. During the summer-time, it was one continuous round of war-parties going out to attack their enemies, and parties returning, bringing with them the scalps of those they had killed, together with squaws and children they had captured, and frequently with large herds of horses they had stolen. If the raids were against the whites, they would return with all sorts of plunder taken from wagon-trains and ranch houses, and oftentimes with captive white women and children. It must be understood that no white man who understood the character of the Indian would ever permit himself to be taken a prisoner, for that meant torture of the most horrible character. For that reason, white men, engaged in battle with the Indians, seldom failed to reserve one last shot in their revolvers, with which to end their lives if capture was imminent, and in many instances men have shot their wives and children rather than allow them to fall into the hands of the Indians. The fate of the women captured by the Indians is indescribable.

After a successful raid, there would ensue a series of scalp dances, accompanied by a period of frenzied rejoicing, in which unspeakable cruelties were perpetrated upon their captive victims. The fiendishness of these cruelties it is almost impossible to describe. In these orgies the squaws always participated, and as a rule were even more diabolical than the warriors. With such examples and with such mothers, how could an Indian child grow up to be anything but fiendish? The Indians had no conception of such a thing as mercy, compassion, or humane treatment of their enemies. Any exhibition of sentiment of that sort would have been considered an evidence of weakness, and any act of forbearance shown toward them by the whites served only to make them more difficult to control thereafter. They gave no quarter and they asked no quarter.

As showing their contempt for the army, I saw upon more than one of the Indian tents that we captured at Sand Creek rude paintings portraying their fights with the soldiers of the United States Army. In every case the soldiers were running at the top of their speed, pursued by Indians who were firing at them and scalping those who had

The Battle of Sand Creek 183

been killed. The Indians knew no law, nor did the Government attempt to teach them any. From the first they were permitted to go on year by year educating their young in savagery, while at the same time the agents of the Government were dealing dishonestly with them; and in every case it was the frontier settler who had to pay the penalty.

The savages soon found out that they could kill the whites, steal or destroy their property throughout the summer, and then upon their professing penitence, the Government would permit them to remain unmolested during the winter and at other times would make a treaty of peace with them and give them large quantities of annuities. After this, they could rest in security until their ponies were in condition to start upon the war-path again the following spring. Was there ever anything in the history of the dealings of any nation with its savage neighbors more absurd or more disreputable? The period I have referred to was certainly a "Century of Dishonor," not only because of the attitude of the Government in its dealings with the Indians, but in the treatment of those of its own people who were opening up frontier lands for settlement.

The Indians could have been easily handled had

the Government studied their nature and formulated a system of laws for their control, compelling them to regard the rights of the whites as well as of their neighboring tribes, and had at the same time protected them from wrongs perpetrated upon them by thieving and disreputable white men; in short, have treated them with justice in all things, and have required the same from them in their dealing with the whites. Had this policy been pursued, it would have been of infinite benefit to the Indians, and would have saved the lives of thousands of white men along the frontier settlements. In this connection, I assert, from my personal knowledge, that more than ninety-five per cent. of the frontier settlers treated the Indians with the utmost fairness and used every possible endeavor to avoid difficulties with them.

As I have already said, the Indian is at a great disadvantage in carrying on warfare during the winter. He has no trouble in this direction in his warfare with his own race, as every tribe is alike in this respect. In this way the white people had a great advantage, and it would have required only a few cases of summary punishment such as we gave them at Sand Creek, to have settled Indian troubles for all time. We who inhabited the frontier in the early sixties knew this and

The Battle of Sand Creek 185

realized that nothing struck such terror to the Indian tribes as to be attacked in the winter, and had the battle of Sand Creek been followed up as it should have been, the frontier settlements of Colorado would thereafter have had little trouble with any of the Indians of the plains.

Four years later, the absurdity of the policy of permitting the Indians to murder and rob during the summer, make peace in the fall, and remain unmolested during the winter, accumulating ammunition for the following summer's warfare, finally dawned upon the military authorities and a new policy was adopted. As a result, on the 27th of November, 1868, General Custer, under the direction of General Sheridan, commander of the military division of the Missouri, made an attack upon the Cheyennes camped on the Washita, south of the Arkansas River, in which one hundred and three Indians (a number of whom were squaws) were killed, fifty-three squaws and children were captured, and 875 ponies were taken. This attack was at the same time of year and was almost identical with that made by Chivington at Sand Creek. General Sheridan says in his report:

The objects of the winter's operations were to strike a hard blow and force them on to the reservation set apart for them, or if this could not be accomplished, to show to the Indian that the winter season would not give him rest; that he, with his village and stock, could be destroyed; that he would have no security winter or summer except in obeying the laws of peace and humanity.

As in the case of Chivington, Custer was attacked viciously for this affair by Wynkoop and others, but, fortunately, Custer had the backing of the commanding officers of the army and nothing his enemies could do affected him in the least.

What a fortunate thing it would have been for the frontier people if this policy had been adopted a few years sooner!

CHAPTER VII

THE INDIAN WAR OF 1868

DURING the three years following the battle of Sand Creek there was little trouble with the Indians in El Paso County; consequently the people of that section of Colorado, while keeping a sharp lookout, felt fairly safe upon their ranches. During the summer season of each of these years, however, the Sioux, Cheyennes, and Arapahoes continued their raids upon the exposed settlements and the lines of travel to the East.

In the meantime, the Government was following its usual temporizing policy with the savages. In the spring of 1867, agents of the Indian Bureau attempted to negotiate a new treaty with the Cheyennes and Arapahoes, and for that purpose visited them at their camp on Pawnee Fork, near Fort Larned, Kansas. But spring was not the time of year when the Indians wanted to negotiate treaties, and as a result, after making several appointments for councils, none of which was kept, the savages suddenly disappeared, and were next heard of raiding the frontier settlements of Kansas and Nebraska, and the lines of travel between Colorado and the Missouri River. These raids were continued during the next five or six months, but, after killing and robbing the whites all summer, these Cheyennes and Arapahoes came in again professing penitence; whereupon, following the usual custom, a new treaty was made with them, by the terms of which both tribes consented to give up their lands in Colorado and settle upon a reservation elsewhere. Under the treaty, they agreed that "hereafter they would not molest any coach or wagon, nor carry off any white woman or child, nor kill or scalp any white man." For this and the lands ceded by them, these tribes were to receive twenty thousand dollars annually, and a suit of clothes for each Indian; and, in addition, teachers, physicians, farmers' implements, etc., were to be provided, in order to help them to acquire the habits of civilization.

While it was not expressly stated in the treaty, it was understood that the Cheyennes and Arapahoes were to be supplied with arms and ammunition. The treaty seems to have been entered into by the agents of the Indian Bureau with all the outward semblance of good faith, although if

The Indian War of 1868

those reponsible knew anything of the facts they must have realized that the promise of these Indians to remain peaceable was utterly worthless, as had been proved year after year for a long period of time. Not only did the treaty turn out to be worthless, but that part of it giving the savages arms and ammunition was particularly reprehensible, as was shown by the results. The savages remained quiet during the winter, as usual, but in the spring they demanded the arms and ammunition that had been promised to them, and the Indian agents urged the Bureau to grant the request, making the plea that the Indians would starve unless these were given to them, so that they might be able to hunt the buffalo and other game of the plains.

Evidently the Government hesitated, but, finally, influenced by these statements, the issue of the arms and ammunition was authorized. At this juncture, Major Wynkoop, who after the battle of Sand Creek had proved himself an enemy of the people of Colorado, again showed that he had no regard for their welfare. He had by this time been taken into the service of the Indian Bureau, presumably as a reward for his services in aid of the Bureau in connection with the Sand Creek investigation, and had been appointed an Indian agent. He was one of those who had been urging that arms and ammunition be given to the Indians, and it was he who finally delivered them to the savages. On August 10, 1868, he wrote to the Department:

I yesterday made the whole issue of annuity, goods, arms, and ammunition to the Cheyenne chiefs and people of their nation. They were delighted in receiving the goods, *particularly the arms and ammunition*, and never before have I known them to be better satisfied and express themselves as being so well contented previous to the issue. They have now left for their hunting grounds and I am perfectly satisfied that there will be no trouble with them this season.

On the very day that Wynkoop sent this letter, a body of two hundred and fifty Cheyennes, Arapahoes, and Sioux were raiding the settlements on the Saline River in Kansas, killing settlers, burning buildings, and committing unspeakable outrages on many defenseless women. Before the end of the month, according to the report of General Sheridan for that year, forty white men had been killed by the savages on the frontiers of Kansas and Colorado, many were wounded, and a large amount of property destroyed.

I must, however, confine my narrative to

events that occurred in El Paso County and the counties adjoining. About ten days after the Wynkoop letter was written, a party of seventy-five Cheyennes and Arapahoes, all well mounted, marched in from the plains and passed up through Colorado City. Most of the savages had modern guns and were well supplied with ammunition,—presumably issued by the Government. They bore letters from Indian agents and peace commissioners, which stated that they were peaceably disposed and should not be feared nor molested; but our people, not being satisfied with that kind of testimony, telegraphed to the Governor at Denver, who replied, reiterating that they were not hostile and must not be interfered with. At the time of their visit to Colorado City, the Indians were noticeably sullen in their demeanor, and appeared to be observing everything in a suspicious manner. However, they left without committing any overt act, and, apparently, went on leisurely up the Ute Pass into the mountains to fight the Utes, which they claimed was their intention.

A day or two later they surprised a small band of Utes who were camped a few miles south of the Hartsell ranch in the South Park, and in the fight that followed claimed to have killed six of the Utes including two or three squaws, and to have carried off a small boy. On the day of this occurrence Samuel Hartsell, owner of the ranch above referred to, had gone over to the mountains that form the eastern border of the South Park, looking for wild raspberries. While on one of the low mountains of that locality, he saw a group of mounted men in the valley below, a mile or so away. He had not heard of any Cheyennes or Arapahoes being in that neighborhood, consequently he very naturally concluded that the horsemen were Utes. Having been on friendly terms with that tribe for many years, and well acquainted with many of its members, he decided to ride down the mountain to meet them. But as he came near the group, he noticed that they were not dressed as the Utes usually were, nor did they look like the people of that tribe; however, it was now too late to retreat, as almost immediately afterward he was discovered and surrounded by the savages. By that time Hartsell, through his general knowledge of the Indians of this Western country, knew that his captors were Cheyenne and Arapahoe warriors, tribes that had been hostile to the whites during the past four years, and were still hostile, so far as he knew. Consequently, he was very much alarmed, realizing that he was in a very dangerous situation. Evidently, the savages were not yet ready to begin hostilities, as was proved by their efforts to reassure Hartsell by showing him their certificates from Indian agents, telling of their peaceable character; but this did not prevent them from at once taking his revolver, ammunition, and pocket knife.

Hartsell estimated that there were about seventy Indians in the band, all of whom were fully armed and amply supplied with ammunition. The savages told him of their victory over the Utes, showed him the scalps they had taken, and the boy they had captured. Finally, after keeping Hartsell in suspense for more than three hours, the Indians allowed him to go without injury, and then departed eastward in the direction of Colorado City. The people of Colorado City and its vicinity knew nothing of this occurrence until some time afterwards. Notwithstanding the assurance of the Governor and the Indian agents, the settlers continued to be very much alarmed at the presence of the savages, and knowing their treacherous nature, maintained a sharp lookout in order to prevent being attacked unawares. About eleven o'clock in the morning three or four days after the savages disappeared up Ute Pass, three Indians appeared at H. M. Teachout's ranch on Monument Creek, eight miles northeast of Colorado City. They claimed to be friendly Utes, but Teachout, being familiar with the Indian tribes of the region, knew that they were not Utes. After staying five or ten minutes, during which time they seemed to be intent on taking in the surroundings, and especially the corral where Teachout's large herd of horses was kept at night, they left, following the main road towards Colorado City. Mr. Teachout and his brother, who lived on the Divide, owned about one hundred and fifty horses, all of which were kept at this Monument Creek ranch.

After the Indians had disappeared, Teachout, being alarmed, rounded up his horses and drove them into the corral, where he kept them during the daytime thereafter, letting them out to graze only at night, thinking that the safest plan. Apparently, the Indians, having obtained all the information they desired concerning the settlements around Colorado City, disappeared, and a day or two later were heard of raiding the frontier settlements east of Bijou Basin and on the headwaters of Kiowa, Bijou, and Running creeks, during which raid they killed several people and ran off much stock.

The Indian War of 1868

On August 27, 1868, the Cheyennes and Arapahoes killed Mrs. Henrietta Dieterman and her five-year-old son on Comanche Creek, about twenty-five miles northeast of Colorado City, in a peculiarly atrocious manner. The Dieterman household consisted of Mr. and Mrs. Dieterman, a daughter about twelve years old, a son of five years, a sister of Mr. Dieterman's, and a hired man. The sister was soon to marry the hired man, and he and Mr. Dieterman had gone to Denver to buy furniture for the new household, leaving a German farmhand temporarily in charge. On the morning of the 27th, something happened to alarm Mrs. Dieterman. She evidently believed the Indians were near, for she hurriedly started with her sister-in-law and the two children for a neighbor's house some distance away. After having gone a few hundred yards she remembered that she had left a considerable sum of money in the house, and with her small son went back to get it. They reached the house, got the money, and started away again, but had gone only a short distance when they were overtaken by the Indians, who at once shot and killed both of them. The savages shot the boy repeatedly and finally broke his neck. The mother was shot through the body, stabbed, and scalped, and the bodies of both were dreadfully mutilated. Those who afterwards saw the victims said that it was one of the most horrible sights they had ever looked upon. Meanwhile, the sister-in-law and daughter ran to where the German was working in the field near by. He stood the Indians off by pointing the handle of his hoe at them, making them believe it was a gun. In that way he covered the retreat of himself and the others to a neighbor's house. Mrs. Dieterman had formerly lived near the northern line of El Paso County, and was well known to many of the old settlers. The awful tragedy of her death created a great sensation, not only in that county, but also in Denver and throughout the entire State. News of the killing of Mrs. Dieterman and of the other outrages perpetrated by the Indians in that region reached Colorado City late in the evening, a day or two afterwards. As there was a possibility of the savages appearing at any moment, messengers were at once sent throughout the county notifying the people of the great danger that confronted them. At that time I happened to be at home with my father and other members of the family on our Bear Creek ranch. About eleven o'clock at night, we were aroused from sleep by the messenger sent to warn us and were advised to

The Indian War of 1868

go immediately to Colorado City for protection. We appreciated the danger of our situation and quickly hitched up our team, put a few necessary articles of wearing apparel and bedding into the wagon, and started for town, three miles distant. It was a dark night, which made the trip a weird as well as an anxious one. With my sisters and younger brothers in the wagon, my father and I marched along behind, each with a rifle in hand, knowing that there was a possibility that the Indians had already stolen into this region, and that every bush or rock on the way might conceal a savage; but nothing happened and we reached town in safety. It was an incident that made one appreciate to the fullest extent the disagreeable and dangerous features of frontier life. We rented a house in Colorado City, moved our household effects from the ranch, and remained in town until after the Indian troubles were over.

Early in the morning of September 1st, Mr. Teachout, accompanied by his hired man, went out to bring in his herd of horses, as had been his custom since the visit of the three Indians a few days previous. They went down Monument Creek a mile or two, then up Cottonwood Creek, where they found the herd scattered along the valley for a mile or more above the point where the Santa Fé Railway now crosses that creek, which is about six miles north of the present city of Colorado Springs. The two rode leisurely through the herd up the valley on the south side of the stream, and had gone about half a mile above the point just mentioned, when they saw a half dozen mounted Indians come over the hill to the north and dash at full speed in the direction of the herd. Following them, other Indians came in sight, until there were at least twenty-five in the band. In a very short time the savages had rounded up most of the horses and were driving them up the creek at a furious speed. They passed Teachout, who was on the other side of the creek, expecting every minute to be attacked. Neither he nor his hired man had guns, but as they did not run, the Indians evidently thought they were armed, and kept some distance away. As they went by, one of the Indians who could speak English yelled: "Damn you, we are going to take your horses!" Soon after this, Teachout saw that the Indians had missed a bunch of fifteen to twenty colts that were grazing off to one side, and he and his hired man started after them, thinking to save at least that part of the herd. But the Indians soon discovered what they were after and started in pursuit, firing as they went. When affairs took this turn, there was nothing left for Teachout and his man to do but ride for their lives, and get back to the ranch as quickly as possible, which they did. The Indians rounded up the colts and soon disappeared to the eastward up Cottonwood Creek with the entire herd. Less than an hour afterward, they passed a ranch near the head of the creek, traveling rapidly. At this place the Indians attempted to add to their herd, but failed, as the horses they were after happened to be picketed close to the house, and a few shots from two well-armed ranchmen entrenched behind the walls of their log cabin drove the savages off.

Upon reaching home, Teachout immediately sent a messenger to his brother on the Divide, with an account of the raid and a request that he enlist as large an armed force as could quickly be gotten together, to follow the Indians and, if possible, recover the horses. The brother acted promptly, and that evening a party consisting of Dow and Bale Simpson, Jim Sims, "Wild Bill," and others, whose names I have been unable to obtain, twenty-eight in all, started in pursuit of the savages. The party camped that night at a ranch about three miles southeast of C. R. Husted's saw-mill, and at this point were joined by a Mr. Davis and Job Talbert, a brother-in-law of Mr. Husted. These two men had expected to get horses and arms at this ranch. Failing in this, however, they started back to the mill the following morning, but had gone only a short distance when the Indians overtook them, killed and scalped both leaving their mutilated bodies in the road, where they were found by their friends a few hours afterward.

The Simpson party, as it afterwards was called, started again early in the morning, soon found the trail of the captured herd, and followed it rapidly along the south side of the pinery, then eastward across Squirrel Creek and down the Big Sandy to the mouth of a creek coming in from the north, the size of the herd making the trail plain and easy to follow. So far no Indians had been seen, and the indications were that the Indians with the stolen horses were so far ahead as to make further pursuit useless. But instead of returning directly home, they decided to follow up this creek and scout the country to the east of Bijou Basin. A few miles up the creek they came to a ranch, which they found deserted. The house was open and had been thoroughly ransacked, but the owner nowhere appeared. After considerable search, his dead body was found some distance away.

The Indian War of 1868

He had been killed and scalped by the Indians, and, as in every other case, the body had been horribly mutilated, the house looted, and all his stock driven off. After burying the body, the party continued in a northerly direction until it reached the old Smoky Hill road. Here they met a party of eighteen men from the country to the north of Bijou Basin, and it was decided to combine the two forces for further scouting in that region. A short distance away from their camp that night, they found and buried the bodies of two men who had been killed by the Indians a day or two before. The combined parties camped together that night, and the following morning started towards Bijou Basin. During all this time no Indians had been seen, and it seemed probable that the savages had returned to their villages on the plains. Under this impression, the men marched rather carelessly along, strung out over the prairie for a considerable distance. Early in the afternoon the party of eighteen, having decided that there was nothing further they could accomplish, left the Simpson party and started off northwesterly, in the direction of their homes. Hardly were they out of sight when two of Simpson's men, who were some distance ahead of the main party, saw a few Indians on a hill not very far away. Word was at once sent back to the stragglers, and the party closed up in double-quick time. Meanwhile other Indians appeared, until in a short time they greatly outnumbered the Simpson party. This made it imperative that a place for defense should be found without delay. Apparently, the most favorable position in sight was the extreme point of a short and rather isolated ridge near by, at which place the ground dropped off rather abruptly on three sides. The men rushed to this point, formed a circle, and began to throw up temporary entrenchments with butcher knives and such other implements as they had at hand. By this time the Indians, under cover of a ridge to the south, had opened a sharp fire. Bullets were whizzing around in a lively fashion and in a few minutes several of the horses had been wounded. However, an encouraging feature of the situation was that many of the shots fired by the Indians struck the ground some distance away. The whites returned the fire at every opportunity, and had reason to believe that their shots had been effective in a number of instances, although the Indians kept under cover as much as possible. Before darkness came on, a number of Simpson's men had been wounded and several of the horses killed. By this time, notwithstanding the strong defense that was being made, it became more and more a question whether the party could withstand a vigorous charge by the Indians.

Night coming on, the firing of the Indians slackened a little and the men were enabled to give some consideration to their situation. It was realized that neither their location nor resources were favorable for a long siege, and for that reason help must be obtained as soon as possible. Among the party was a dare-devil sort of fellow known by the name of "Wild Bill," who volunteered to take the fastest horse, and in the darkness endeavor to break through the Indian line, which now completely surrounded the hill. Then, if successful, he was to hurry on to the settlements at Bijou Basin, fifteen miles away, and bring back reinforcements as quickly as possible. This suggestion met with the approval of every one, and arrangements were immediately made to carry it into effect. About nine o'clock Wild Bill, mounted on Dow Simpson's race horse, stole out from the entrenchments and quietly rode away. The night being moderately dark, he succeeded in getting some distance away before he was discovered by the Indians. He then put spurs to his horse and dashed away at the best speed the animal was capable of, the Indians following in a frantic endeavor to cut him off, shooting at him as they ran. Fortunately neither he nor the horse was hit, and in a short time he had left the Indians far behind. After that, he was not long in reaching Bijou Basin, where arrangements were at once made to dispatch couriers to Colorado City and elsewhere for reinforcements.

Meanwhile, those surrounded on the hill were most anxious for the safety of their messenger. They heard the shots and knew that he had been discovered, and that the Indians were in pursuit of him, but had no means of telling whether or not he had escaped. The only reassuring circumstance was that soon after this the firing gradually slackened, finally stopping altogether; and when daylight came there were no Indians in sight. The besieged men realized that this might be only a ruse, and that possibly the Indians were lurking near, ready to take advantage of them after they had left their entrenchments. However, on account of their critical position, being entirely without water for themselves and their horses, they determined to make a dash and take a chance of reaching the settlements. This being decided upon, they started at once, and without further

The Indian War of 1868

molestation reached Holden's ranch in Bijou Basin before noon, no Indians having been seen on the way. In the engagement none of the party had been killed and no one seriously wounded, probably because of the poor ammunition issued to the Indians by the Government—for which I suppose the white people of this region should have been duly thankful.

While this engagement had been going on, stirring events had been happening in the neighborhood of Colorado City and elsewhere in the county. As I have already stated, within the next few days after the killing of Mrs. Dieterman, and the raid upon Teachout's horses, most of the ranchmen down the Fountain Valley had brought their families to Colorado City for protection. The people of the Divide gathered for defense at McShane's ranch near Monument, at John Irion's on Cherry Creek, and at Husted's mill in the pinery. The air was full of rumors of Indian depredations in every direction; but, as it was harvest time, it was imperative that the gathering of the crops be attended to. This made it necessary that some chances be taken, and it so happened that, when the crisis came, many of the men of Colorado City were out in the harvest fields of the surrounding country.

About noon on September 3, 1868, a band of forty to fifty Indians came dashing down the valley of Monument Creek, capturing all loose horses in their path. The first white man they ran across was Robert F. Love, of Colorado City, who was riding along the higher ground to the east of Monument Creek, not far from the present town of Roswell. As soon as Love saw the Indians, instead of trying to get away, which he knew would be useless, he dismounted, keeping his pony between himself and the savages, and, by keeping his revolver pointed in their direction, showing them that he was armed. After maneuvering around him for a time, the Indians passed on, apparently convinced that some of them would get hurt if they remained. It was not their policy to take many chances, as was evidenced throughout their entire stay in this region. They seldom troubled people who seemed to offer any serious resistance, seeking rather defenseless men, women, and children. Soon after leaving Love, a few of the Indians crossed Monument Creek to the house of David Spielman, which stood on the west side, about half a mile above the Mesa Road Bridge in the present city of Colorado Springs. Spielman had just finished moving his family and household effects to Colorado City, and being

The Indian War of 1868

tired, had lain down behind the open front door, and had gone to sleep. The Indians looked in at the open door, but fortunately did not see him. They then went to the corral and took from it a horse that Spielman had purchased only the day before. After that they recrossed Monument Creek and joined the main body, which continued rapidly along the low ground east of the creek, crossing the present Washburn Athletic Field, on the way, and coming out on to the higher ground a few hundred yards south of Cutler Academy, near where the Hagerman residence now stands.

A short time previously, Charley Everhart, a young man about eighteen years of age, had started from his home just west of Monument Creek and near the present railway bridge above the Rio Grande station, to look after his father's cattle, that were grazing on the plain now covered by the city of Colorado Springs. After crossing Monument Creek, he followed a trail that led eastward along the south rim of the high bank north of what is now known as Boulder Crescent. Everhart knew there were Indians in the country, and was no doubt on the lookout for them. He was mounted on a small pony, and had probably gone as far east as the present location of Tejon Street, when he evidently saw the Indians as they came out into open view to the north of him. He at once turned his pony toward home and urged it to its highest speed, making a desperate effort to escape from the savages; but his horse was no match for those of the Indians, and they soon overtook him. Everhart had reached a point near the intersection of what is now Platte and Cascade Avenues, when a shot from one of the savages caused him to fall from his horse. One of the Indians then came up to him, ran a spear through his body, and scalped him, taking all the hair from his head except a small fringe around the back part. The whole occurrence was witnessed from a distance by several persons. An hour or so afterward, when the Indians had gone and it was safe to do so, a party went out to where his mutilated body lay, and brought it to Colorado City.

After killing Everhart, the Indians saw farther down the valley, a quarter of a mile or so away, a lone sheep herder, who was generally known as "Judge" Baldwin, and the whole band immediately started after him. When Baldwin saw the Indians coming, he tried to escape. Having no spurs or whip, he took off one of his long-legged boots and used it to urge his mount to its utmost speed. This, however, was ineffectual, as his

The Indian War of 1868   209

horse was inferior to those of the Indians, and they had no difficulty in overtaking him before he had gone very far. They shot him, and he fell from his horse near the site of the present Fourth Ward Schoolhouse. The bullet struck Baldwin in the shoulder, and as he was leaning forward at the time, it passed upward through his neck and came out through the jaw. He dropped from his horse completely dazed, but in his delirium he used the boot to fight off the Indians. The latter evidently thought the wound mortal, so without wasting any more ammunition upon him one of their number proceeded to take his scalp. The savage ran the knife around the back part of Baldwin's head, severing the scalp from the skull, and then discovered that he had been scalped at some previous time. For some reason, probably superstition of some kind, the Indians then abandoned the idea of scalping him, and the entire band rode off, leaving their victim, as they supposed, to die on the prairie. It was a fact that Baldwin had been scalped by Indians in South America some years before.

After leaving Baldwin, the Indians divided into two bands, one of which went in a northeasterly direction and crossed Shooks Run near the point where Platte Avenue now intersects it. Near this place they were joined by other Indians who had evidently been in concealment near by. It is said that during all this time two or three Indians stationed on the hill where the Deaf and Blind Institute is now located, apparently by the use of flags, directed the movements of those doing the killing, wigwagging in a manner similar to that in use in the army at that time, and that these signal men fell in with the others as they came along; after which they all rode rapidly to the eastward and soon disappeared on the plains. The other party continued down the valley of the Fountain, and at a point just below where the Rio Grande bridge now crosses Shooks Run, they came upon two small boys, the sons of Thomas H. Robbins, who lived on the south side of the Fountain, not far away. These two boys, eight and ten years of age respectively, were looking after their father's cattle. They had evidently seen the Indians coming when some distance away, as they were using every possible endeavor to escape; but they had not gone far when the savages were upon them. It is said that one of the boys fell upon his knees and lifted up his hands, as though begging the Indians to spare his life, but the savages never heeded such appeals. Two Indians reached down, each seized a boy by the hair, held him up with one hand, and, using a revolver, shot him with the other and then flung the quivering, lifeless body to the ground.

The savages then continued rapidly down along the edge of the bluffs, to the north of Fountain Creek, and when at the south side of the present Evergreen Cemetery, attempted to capture some horses at the Innis ranch, in the valley a short distance away, but the presence of a number of armed men there caused them to desist after two or three futile dashes in that direction. Half a mile below this point, they met Solon Mason, a ranchman from the lower end of the county, accompanied by two or three other men. These men were all armed and, after two or three shots were exchanged, the Indians gave them a wide berth. At a ranch just below, occupied by George Banning, the Indians secured a few horses, after which they struck out over the plains to join the other band.

As I have already said, armed parties were going out every day from Colorado City to harvest the grain that had been ripe for some time. On that morning, I had joined a group that was to assist Bert Myers, a merchant of Colorado City, in harvesting a field of wheat on land now occupied by the town of Broadmoor. I was binding wheat behind a reaper, at a point not very far from the present Country Club buildings, when, about two o'clock in the afternoon, I saw a horseman coming from the east riding furiously in our direction. When he reached us we found that it was a Mr. Riggs, who lived near the mouth of Cheyenne Creek. He told us that the Indians were raiding the settlements in every direction, and were killing people, mentioning of his own knowledge Everhart, Baldwin, and the Robbins boys, and he thought a good many more; and also had run off a large number of horses. My first thought was that the Indians had come in during the previous night, concealed themselves in the underbrush along the creeks, and taken advantage of the time when most of the men were out in the fields, to attack, rob, and murder. I knew such a thing was possible, as there was no one living between our settlement and the Indian country to give us notice of the approach of a hostile band. It then occurred to me that my three small brothers, Edgar, Frank, and Charles, were looking after our cattle near the mouth of Bear Creek, and certainly were in great danger, if indeed they had not already been killed. I immediately secured permission to take one of the horses from the reaper, in order to ride in search

The Indian War of 1868

of the boys. I quickly stripped off all the harness except the blind bridle, mounted the horse, and tore away in the direction of Bear Creek. As a matter of precaution, I had taken a revolver with me to the harvest-field as at this time few went out unarmed. After a ride at top speed, I met the boys about three-quarters of a mile south of Bear Creek.

My brothers told me that while eating their luncheon in the milk house near our dwelling on Bear Creek, they were alarmed by the excited barking of their dog. They ran out to see what was the matter, and, looking across on the present site of Colorado Springs, saw a group of horsemen whom they immediately knew to be Indians, pursuing another horseman, whom they at once conjectured was Charley Everhart. A moment later the band seemed to be grouped around some object, which doubtless was the time when the Indians were scalping young Everhart. The boys witnessed the savages race down over the flat in their pursuit of Baldwin, and while this was in progress, they counted the horsemen and found that there were thirty-five in the band. The boys then ran up the hill to the east of the house, heard the shot, and witnessed what I have already described concerning the shooting of Baldwin. They then saw the band divide, one party going out on the plains and the other down the creek. Becoming alarmed for their own safety, they had started to run to some of the neighbors on Cheyenne Creek, when I met them. As soon as I had heard their story, which assured me that the Indians had gone off to the east and that there was no immediate danger to the boys, I rode back to the harvest-field where we had abandoned the reaper, hitched to the wagon, and drove to town. Later in the afternoon, the Robbins family, whose two boys had been killed, as I have related, came by our Bear Creek ranch on their way to Colorado City, and took my brothers to town with them. By the time we reached Colorado City, the bodies of Everhart and the two Robbins boys had been brought in. The party that went after Baldwin found him alive, but supposed him to be mortally wounded. It was thought that he could not possibly live more than a day or two at most, but, to the surprise of everybody, in a short time he began to recover and in a month or so was apparently well again.

Of course, the excitement in Colorado City and throughout the county was intense. We knew that the Territorial authorities were unable to give us any help whatsoever, and that the general

The Indian War of 1868

Government had turned a deaf ear to our appeals for protection. Consequently, we realized that we must again, as in 1864, rely solely upon ourselves. In this emergency we repaired the old fort around the log hotel, and organized our forces to the best possible advantage, in order to be prepared for any further attacks that the Indians might make. Only a few hours after the raid, a messenger came in from Bijou Basin, asking that men be sent to the relief of the Simpson party, which was surrounded by Indians near that point, as I have already told. After consideration of the matter, it was decided that our force was strong enough to spare a few men for that purpose. Accordingly, that night ten of us volunteered to go to the assistance of the besieged. For this expedition a Mr. Hall, who lived on what has since been known as the Pope ranch, loaned me an excellent horse and a Colt's rifle, a kind of gun I had never seen before nor have I seen one like it since. It was a gun built exactly on the principle of a Colt's revolver, the only trouble with it being that one never knew just how many shots would go off at once.

Early the following morning we started out, following up Monument Creek to the mouth of Cottonwood; thence up that creek over the ground where Teachout's herd of horses had been captured. We stopped a few minutes at the Neff ranch, which we found deserted, and then went east along the route taken by the Indians when running off the Teachout herd.

An hour later, while we were riding along in a leisurely manner, and had reached within about half a mile of the pinery, we saw to our right a band of about twenty-five mounted Indians, half a mile away on the south bank of Cottonwood Creek. We had been so wrought up by the murders of the previous day, that without a moment's hesitation we wheeled about and made for the Indians as fast as our horses could go. We had no sooner started than I realized that we might be running into an ambuscade, and I warned our people not to cross the ravine at the place where we had first seen the savages, but to go on one side or the other; however, our men were in such a state of frenzy, that they would not listen, so we rushed headlong to the bank of the ravine through which the creek ran. The bank was so steep that we had to dismount and lead our horses. Fortunately for us, there were no Indians at that moment at the point where we were crossing the ravine, but we had not gone a quarter of a mile before a mounted Indian appeared on the bank,

The Indian War of 1868

almost at that identical place, and probably there were others hidden near the same point.

As soon as the Indians on the south bank saw us coming, they started on the run in a southeasterly direction, and, when some distance away, gradually turned to the eastward. By this time our party began to think a little of the desirability of keeping a way of retreat open, in case of defeat in the expected engagement. For that reason, we veered a little to the right, and kept on until we were directly between them and Colorado City. By this time, the Indians had dismounted on a large open flat, about three-quarters of a mile to the eastward of us, and, forming a circle with their ponies, seemed to be awaiting our attack. We could see their guns flashing in the sunshine, and while we were surprised at this movement, so contrary to the usual custom of the Indians, we did not hesitate a moment, but started toward them as fast as our ponies could take us. Evidently changing their minds upon seeing this, the Indians remounted and started in the direction of the pinery as rapidly as they could go. Their horses were better and fleeter than ours, so we were unable to head them off, and when they entered the edge of the timber we knew it would only be inviting disaster to follow farther. We then resumed our march in the direction of Bijou Basin. An hour or two later, we went by the extreme eastern edge of the pinery, at the point where the old government road crossed Squirrel Creek. Here, judging by the great number of fresh pony tracks, a large number of Indians must have passed only a short time previously. After a short rest at this point, we rode steadily on and reached Bijou Basin that evening just before dark. On our arrival, we found that the besieged party had come in the day before, and that all the men, except the wounded, had returned to their homes. The wounded were being cared for at Mr. D. M. Holden's ranch. There being nothing further for us to do, we started for home early the following morning. Upon our way, we found many Indian pony tracks at various places along the eastern and southern edge of the pinery, showing that the Indians were still around in considerable numbers, but we saw none during the day. After leaving the pinery, we followed the wagon road that came down through what is now known as the Garden Ranch. As we came down the hill, two or three miles to the northeast of the ranch houses, we noticed a number of horsemen congregated near that point. From their actions we knew that they were very much excited, and evidently mistook us for a band of Indians. They gathered around some tall rocks a little way to the eastward of the gateway, and seemed to be preparing for defense. We tried by signaling and otherwise to make ourselves known to them, but were unsuccessful until we were almost within gun-shot distance. They were greatly relieved when they ascertained who we were. We then joined them and reached Colorado City without further incident.

Events of a similar character were of almost daily occurrence while the Indians remained in this region. Every animal on a distant hill became an Indian horseman to the excited imagination of the ranchman or cowboy, and without further investigation he rushed off to town to give the alarm. No lone man on horseback allowed another horseman to approach him without preparing for defense, and every object at a distance that was not clearly distinguishable was viewed with alarm.

For two weeks following the raid upon the present town-site of Colorado Springs, the Indians had virtual possession of the northern and eastern portions of the county. During this time they raided Gill's ranch, east of Jimmy's Camp, and ran off his herd of horses, taking them out of the corral near his house in the night, although the horses were being guarded by armed men. It appears that the Indians stole up to the corral on the opposite side from where the guards were posted, made an opening in it, let the horses out, and were off with them before the men realized what was going on.

About the same time, the Indians killed a demented man named Jonathan Lincoln, at the Lincoln ranch in Spring Valley on Cherry Creek, just north of the El Paso County line. Lincoln and a Mexican were out in the harvest-field binding oats when they saw the Indians approaching. The Mexican saved himself by flight, but Lincoln folded his arms and calmly awaited the coming of the savages. Without hesitation they killed him, took his scalp, and departed again into the recesses of the adjacent pinery. They also killed John Choteau, on east Cherry Creek, John Grief and Jonathan Tallman on east Bijou, and raided the John Russell ranch at the head of East Cherry Creek, from which place they ran off sixteen horses.

About this time, a small band of Indians, while prowling around near the town of Monument, threatened the house of David McShane at a time when all the men were away, Mrs. McShane and some neighboring women and children being the only occupants. Having the true pioneer spirit, the women, under the leadership of Mrs. McShane, put up such a strong show of defense that the savages abandoned the attack in short order, apparently glad to get away unharmed. Soon after, they burned Henry Walker's house, which stood about a mile east of the present Husted station on the Denver and Rio Grande Railroad.

The Indians seemed to have established a camp at some secluded place in the timber of the Divide, from which they went out in small parties in every direction, killing and robbing when opportunity offered. Every day during these two weeks, Indians were seen at various places on the Divide and the eastern part of the county. By this time, however, our people had taken their families out of danger and were so constantly on the alert that the Indians, while having many opportunities for looting and robbing the deserted ranches, had few chances for surprising and killing defenseless people, who were the only ones they cared to attack. Throughout the raid, those who had been able to make any kind of a defense had been let alone. The Indians seemed unwilling to take any chances or to waste their ammunition, unless they were certain of results.

A week or two after the beginning of the Indian

troubles, the people of El Paso County took steps to form a military company to be regularly employed against the Indians, its members to serve without pay. It was the intention to keep this company in the field until the Indians were driven out of the region. About the fifteenth of September, eighty mounted and well-armed men, who had enlisted for the purpose, and of whom I was one, met at Husted's saw-mill on the Divide and perfected a military organization by the election of the usual company officers, A. J. Templeton being elected captain. The company took up its line of march through the pinery to Bijou Basin; thence eastward past the place where Simpson's party had been besieged two or three weeks before. After examining with much interest the scene of this fight, we went southeasterly to Big Sandy Creek, thence down the valley of that creek to Lake Station on the Smoky Hill wagon road, about ten miles east of the present town of Limon. On our march we saw no Indians, and, judging from their trails and from other indications, we decided that they were leaving the country. As we marched down the valley of the Big Sandy, in the vicinity of the present towns of Ramah and Calhan, we saw hundreds of dead cattle, most of them cows that had been killed by

The Indian War of 1868

the Indians only a day or two before. That these cattle had been wantonly killed, was shown by the fact that no part of the animals had been taken for food. In almost every instance they had been shot with arrows, many of which were at the time sticking in the carcasses. Besides the dead cattle, we saw hundreds of live ones scattered all over the hills and down the valley, which had evidently been driven off by the Indians from the ranches in El Paso and the surrounding counties. At a point about ten miles down the valley from the present station of Limon, on the Rock Island Railway, the trail of the Indians left the valley and turned northeastward. At this place we were about seventy-five miles southwest from the Beecher Island battle ground, on the Arickaree fork of the Republican River, where Colonel George A. Forsyth and his fifty followers were at that very time making their heroic defense against an overwhelming number of Indians under the command of the famous chief Roman Nose, although we knew nothing of the affair until some time later. The trail of the Indians led across the country in a direct line toward the battle ground. No doubt they had been summoned by runners to aid their people, and probably this was the reason for their leaving El Paso County.

Upon discovering the course taken by the Indians, Captain Templeton, on account of his small force, deemed it imprudent to pursue them farther. An additional reason for facing about was that our supply of provisions was about exhausted, and had we gone farther we should have had to subsist on the wild game of the region, which would have been a risky thing to attempt. As it was, on our way homeward we had to live entirely on the meat of cattle we killed. Having no camp outfit, we broiled the meat on sticks before our camp fires and then ate it without salt. To me this fare was about the nearest to a starvation diet that I have ever experienced. We reached Colorado City in due time, without having seen an Indian during our whole campaign. Whether we were the cause of the Indians leaving this region, or whether it was a coincidence that they were just ahead of us, I do not know, but it was evident that the Indians were gone, and on account of approaching winter we had little to fear from them during the remainder of the year. There apparently being no further use for its services, the company was disbanded.

It had been a strenuous period for the settlers from the first appearance of the Indians about the 20th of August until this time. At least a dozen persons had been killed in El Paso County and the country adjacent thereto on the Divide. Many houses had been destroyed; crops had been lost through inability to harvest the grain; probably five hundred horses and at least one thousand head of cattle had been driven off, making an aggregate loss of property that was extremely heavy for a sparsely populated county such as El Paso was at that time. The contest was an unequal one from the start. The settlers were armed with a miscellaneous lot of guns, most of which were muzzle-loading hunting rifles, while the Indians were armed with breech-loading guns using metal cartridges. Fortunately for the settlers, the ammunition of the Indians was of a poor quality, as was proved in the fight east of Bijou Basin and elsewhere, and, judging by the careful manner in which they used their ammunition, it is probable that the supply was not very large. This undoubtedly saved the lives of many of our people. It was noticed from the first that the Indians never wasted their ammunition and seldom attacked an armed person.

During all the time the savages were going up and down the county murdering people, stealing stock, and destroying the property of the settlers, the general Government did not make the slightest attempt to give our people protection, although attention was repeatedly called to their desperate condition. It is true that a week or two after the Indian troubles began, the Territorial authorities at Denver supplied our people with a limited number of old Belgian muskets, together with the necessary ammunition, but these guns were so much inferior to those in the hands of the Indians, that they were of very little use. With this one exception, the early settlers of this county were left entirely to their own resources from the beginning of the Indian troubles, in 1864, until the end, which did not come until the building of the railroads into the Territory. Every appeal to the general Government for protection was received either with indifference or insult.

In September, 1866, General William T. Sherman, Commander-in-Chief of the United States Army, on his way north from an inspection of the forts in New Mexico, accompanied by a large number of staff officers and a strong escort, stopped overnight in Colorado City. Having been in constant danger from the Indians since the beginning of the trouble in 1864, our people thought this an opportune time to lay the matter before him and ask that proper means of protection be provided. My father, the Rev. Wm. Howbert, was appointed spokesman of the committee that waited upon the General. In his speech, father explained our exposed and defenseless condition, and suggested that a force of government troops be permanently stationed at some point on our eastern frontier, in order to intercept any Indians that might be attempting a raid upon the people of this region. General Sherman received the appeal with utter indifference, and replied that he thought we were unnecessarily alarmed; that there were no hostile Indians in the neighborhood; and then sarcastically remarked that it probably would be a very profitable thing for the people of this region if we could have a force of government troops located near here, to whom our farmers might sell their grain and agricultural products at a high price. With this remark he dismissed the committee, the members of which left the room very indignant at the manner in which their appeal had been received. Later in the year, General Sherman evidently was of the opinion that there *were* hostile Indians in the western country and that they needed severe punishment, for after the massacre of Lieut.-Col. Fetterman and his entire command near Fort Phil Kearny, Wyoming, he telegraphed General Grant, saying: "We must act with vindictive earnestness against the Sioux, even to their extermination, men, women, and children; nothing else will reach the root of the case."

Two years later, in 1868, the General came to Denver along the line of the Kansas-Pacific Railway, at that time under construction, and was glad to have a strong escort to guard him through the region of the hostile Indians. Following this trip, he made a strenuous effort to punish the savages elsewhere, but apparently made no attempt to protect the settlers on the eastern borders of Colorado.

I venture to say that no civilized nation ever gave less attention to protecting its frontier people from the incursion of savages than did our general Government. It was always a question of the influence that could be brought to bear upon the government officials at Washington. After the outbreak of the Indians in Minnesota, in 1862, the Government took prompt measures and punished the savages unmercifully. However, this was due to the fact that Minnesota at that time had two Senators and several members of Congress who were able to bring the necessary influence to bear. During all of our Indian troubles, Colorado had only one delegate in Congress, who had no vote and very little influence.

Consequently, we were left to protect ourselves as best we could.

The whole eastern frontier of El Paso County faced upon the territory occupied by the Sioux, Cheyennes, and Arapahoes, the most crafty and bloodthirsty savages upon the American continent. There were at all times bands of these Indians roaming around on the headwaters of the Republican and Smoky Hill rivers, and it was easy for them to reach the settlements of this county without being observed. Considering these facts, it now seems a wonder that we were not wiped off the face of the earth. Doubtless, as I have said before, the reason that we were not exterminated was the fact of our contiguity to the country of their hereditary enemies, the Utes, for whom, on account of their fighting ability, they had a wholesome respect.

During the Indian troubles, a few settlers left the county and sought places of safety elsewhere, but the great majority of our people pluckily stood their ground. The ranchmen who had brought their families to Colorado City for protection left them there until the trouble was over, but went to their homes as often as they could get two or three armed men to accompany them, to harvest their grain and take care of their stock.

Every time they did this, it was at the risk of their lives, for no one could tell when or where the savages might next appear. The people who now live in the cities and on the ranches of El Paso County can have no true conception of the dangers and the anxieties of the early settlers of the Pike's Peak region. As soon as it was definitely known that the Indians had left the county, most of the ranchmen moved their families back to their homes. From previous experience it was known that, as winter was coming on, there was little danger to be apprehended until the following spring.

By the spring of 1869, the Government, in a winter campaign with troops under the command of General Custer, had administered such severe punishment to the Cheyennes and Arapahoes in the battle of Washita and in other engagements that thereafter the people of El Paso County were unmolested by them, although spasmodic outbreaks occurred at various places out on the plains for several years afterward.

THE END

A Note About This Index

The first edition of The Indians of the Pike's Peak Region (published in 1914) did not have an index. It did not have a foldout map of Territorial Colorado, either. We have added both. The ensuing index was prepared by Miss Katherine McMahon of Albuquerque, N. M. We might make note that as late as 1914, authors were still writing books about frontier America using only surnames or given names without other identification. It is not possible to trace down most of these names, for while a name may be included in the index, the reference could have been so passing or so fleeting no identification is really needed. This index and the foldout map should make this edition more useful and more interesting.

The Publishers

Anthony, Maj. Scott--150-51, 160, 163, 164, 165, 173, 175; testimony, Sand Creek investigation, 151-58
Apache Cañon, N. Mex.--118
Apache (Jicarilla) Indians--2, 3, 4, 20; as hostiles, 126-32 *passim*, 154, 162, 164
Arapahoe Indians--2, 7, 12, 13, 15, 16, 192; dwellings, 23, 24; history, 14; intertribal wars, 19-75 *passim*, as hostiles, 88, 94, 111, 120-74 *passim*,

Arkansas River--10, 13, 49, 55, 59; Indian camps on, 16, 48, 50, 63, 112, 154
Ashcroft, Sam, interpreter--169
Asher Ambrose, Indian captive--127
Ashley, Eli M.--143
Audeby, Jack--62
Baird, William J., pursues Indians--79
Baldwin, "Judge"--208-09, 212, 213-14

Bancroft, Hubert Howe, cited--3, 20
Baxter, Capt. O. H. P.--95, 167, 177
Bayou Salado. *See* South Park
Bear Creek--26, Howbert camp, 196, 212, 213, 214
Beaver Creek ruin, Kans.--3
Bent, George, emissary for Black Kettle--126, 128
Bent, Robert, testimony on Sand Creek battle--
Big Mouth, Indian Chief--150
Big Sandy. *See* Sand Creek battle
Bijou Basin settlers, and Indian raids--200-05, 215, 216, 222, 225
Black Feet Indians--50
Black Hills, So. Dak.--9, 12, 14
Black Kettle, Cheyenne Chief--125, 126, 127, 128, 132, 133, 134, 138, 152, 164, 168, 169, 173
Blue River, captives--127, 133
Blunt, Gen. ___, at Pawnee Fork--159
Boiling Springs. *See* Manitou Springs
Boonville, Colo.--166, 167
Bott, Anthony--64, 79; Colorado Volunteer, 95
Bourgemont, French explorer--9
Buffalo--42, 43, 44, 47

Bull Bear, Cheyenne Chief--134, 136, 138
Cache la Poudre--59, 141
Camp Creek, Howbert camp--77, 78
Canby, Gen. E. R. S.--117
Cañon City, Colo.--48, 55
"Century of Dishonor"--183. *See also* Jackson, Helen Hunt
Chaveno, Ute Chief--73
Cherry Creek, gold found--63; settlers killed, 90, 149
Chever, David A. letter re Sand Creek battle--140-42
Cheyenne Creek, camp ground--24, 25
Cheyenne Indians--2, 7, 12, 13, 15; dwellings, 23, 24; history, 14, "Dog Soldiers", 133, 135
Cheyenne Mountain--46, 47, 48
Chipeta, wife of Ouray--69
Chivington, Col. John. M.--biog. 116, 117; commands Sand Creek battle, 101-13, 151, 154, 167, 167; defense in Sand Creek investigations, 121, 122, 160-66, 172, 173, 175, 178; at Indian councils, 169, 170; as military man, 98, 112, 118, 119, 120, 149-50, 158-59, 185, 186
Choteau, John, killed by Indians--220
Civil War, effect on hostile Indians--93, Appendix II, 364-65

Clayton, Lt.___, and Cheyennes --159
Coby, Henry, Colorado Volunteer--95
Colley, Maj. S.G. Indian Agent--120, 125-26, 129, 133, 135, 163, 164, 165, 166; letter, 130-31; testimony, Sand Creek investigations, 158, 170, 173
Colorado City settlers; build fort, 87; and hostile Indians, 72-92, 191, 193, 194, 195, 196, 197, 199-219, 222-30; isolation, 91, 115
Colorado Springs site--5, 20, 44; and Indian raids, 81, 83, 87, 198, 206, 207
Colorow, Ute Chief--73
Comanche Indians--2, 4, dwellings, 23, 24; history, 9, 10, 11, 13; as hostiles, 126-32 *passim*, 148, 149, 154, 155, 162, 164
Commissioner of Indian Affairs--139, 145; report of 1864, 129, 141, 142; report of 1865, 125-26
Commitee on the Conduct of War, investigations of Sand Creek battle--91, 122, 123, 124, 151, 160, 166
Cone, A.T., pursues Indians --79
Congressional Committee, investigations of Sand Creek battle--121, 122, 127. *See also* Anthony, Maj. Scott, testimony; Chivington, Col. John M. defense; Colley, Maj. S.G., testimony; Evans, Gov. John, defense; Wynkoop, Maj. E.W., testimony
Cottonwood Creek, and Indian raids--197, 199, 215, 216
Cramer, Lt.___--119, 121
Crow Indians--11, 50
Cuartalejo. *See* Quartelejo
Curtis, Gen. S.R.: opposes peace with hostiles--158, 59, 160, 164, 165
Davis, Mr.___, killed by Indians--200
Davis, Capt.___, Calif. Volunteers--155
Delaware Indians--10, 156
Denver, site of--64
Dieterman, Mrs. Henrietta, killed by Indians--195-96, 205
Dodge, Col. Irving, author--47
Early settlers, 1860's--179, 183, 186; isolation of, 85, 86, 93, 115, 141. *See also* Colorado City settlers; El Paso County settlers
Eggleston, Dr.___, pursues Indians--79
Elbert, S.H., defends settlers --171-72
El Paso County Pioneer Society--28

El Paso County settlers, and Indian raids--76, 85, 89, 90, 92
Evans, Gov. John, Adm. of Indian Affairs, Colo. Terr.--123, 131; defense in Sand Creek investigations, 124-46, 172, 173; holds Indian councils, 147-49, 169; prepares against hostiles, 88, 89, 94, 124
Everhart, Charley, killed by Indians--207-08, 212, 213
Ewbanks (Ubanks), Mrs. Lucinda, Indian captive--127, 132
Ewbanks (Ubanks), Isabel, Indian captive--127
Fall Leaf, Delaware Chief--156
Farnham, Thomas J.; describes South Park--48-53
Fetterman, Lt. Col.____, massacred--227
Finley, Robert, Colorado Volunteer--95
First Colorado Cavalry--92, 93, 98, 117, 120, 122, 161, 166, 176, in Sand Creek battle, 101-02
Fontaine qui Bouille Creek country, described--30, 35, 45, 49, 59, 60, 62, 63
Forsyth, Col. George A., and Beecher Island battle--223
Fort Bridger, Wyo.--59
Fort Garland, Colo.--68, 73

Fort Kearney (Kearny), Nebr.--127, 128, 133, 149
Fort Larned, Kans.--131, 153, 154, 159
Fort Lyon, Colo. Indian Agency--99, 122, 125, 131, 134, 145, 150, 153, 154, 162, 165, 166, 167, 168, 171, 173, 179
Fort Lupton, Colo.--69, 90
Fort Napesta, Colo.--67
Fort Phil Kearny, Wyo.--227
Fort Union, N. Mex.--59
Fountain Creek, 26, 27, 71; settlements on, 76, 86, 87, 89, Indian raids, 210, 211
"The Fountain that Boils." *See* Manitou Springs
Frémont, Lt. John C., cited--32-34, 55-57
French explorers--17, 18
French traders--19
Garden of the Gods--27, 78, 79
Garden ranch--218
Gerry, Elbridge, scout--88, 89, 90, 141
Gill's ranch--219
Gold discovered: on Cherry Creek--63; on Platte River, 13
Graham, Lt. Joseph, Colorado Volunteer--95
Great Salt Lake Valley--86
Greeley, Horace, cited--17, 65-67
Grief, John, killed by Indians--220
Hall, Mr.____, early settler--215

Hall, Gen. Frank, *History of Colorado,* cited--71, 118-19
Halleck, Maj. Gen.___, Chief of Staff--159
Hartsell, Samuel, early settler --191, 192
History of Colorado--71, 118-19
Holden's ranch--218
Horse stealing, by Indians--46, 47, 53, 65, 74, 75, 92, 149, 198-200, 216, 217, 211, 216, 219-20
Horses--10, 12, 14, 15
Howbert family--78, 119, 196, 197, 212
Howbert, Rev. Wm.--226-27
Huerfano Creek, Indian raid--68
Hungate family murdered--76, 77, 138, 147
Husted's saw-mill, 199, 205, 222
Indian captives--10, 11, 69, 126, 127, 129, 130, 132, 133, 149, 157-58
Indian Treaties--15-16, 74, 180, 187, 188
James, Dr. Edwin--14, 29-30, 37
James Peak (Pike's Peak)--49
Jimmy's Camp--44, 64, 92, 148, 149
Johnson, Ute Indian--71
Kansas and Pacific Railroad--228
Kiowa Indians--2, 9; dwellings, 23, enemies of Utes, 69;
history, 11, 12, 13; as hostiles, 126-31 *passim,* 148, 149, 154, 155, 162, 164, 166
Left Hand, Arapahoe Chief--65, 125, 127, 133, 150, 152, 158, 168, 174
Limon, Colo.--222, 223
Lincoln, Abraham, and Gov. Evans--123
Lincoln, Jonathan, killed by Indians--220
Little Raven, Arapahoe Chief--153, 157, 174
Long's expedition--14, 21, 44, 49
Loree,___, Indian Agent, report--138
Loup Fork, Nebr.--19
Love, Robert F., early settler --206
McShane's ranch--205, 220-21
Manitou Springs: description of--31, 33, 34, 35, 36; importance to Indians, 29, 30, 32, 37, 58, 60; legend, 10, 38-42
Marble, Daniel, Indian captive--127
Marcy, Col. R.B., cited--59-63
Martin, Mrs.___, Indian captive--133
Mason, Solon, early settler--211
Meeker massacre--71
Methodists--116, 117
Mexico--5, 10

Miller, Henry, Colorado Volunteer--95
Monument Creek: attacks on settlers--194, 197, 206, 207; Indian trail, 27, 29; raiding party, 87, 89, 90
Mukden, the Manchu Home--7
Murray, Samuel, Colorado Volunteer--95
Myers, Bert, merchant--211
Navajo Indians--2
Neva, Arapahoe Chief--128, 152; testimony, 148
New Mexico--1, 2, 3, 4, 8, 9, 19, 59, 86, 155; and Colorado Volunteers, 92, 117, 118, 119
North, Robert, report on hostiles--129-30, 131-32
Norton, Mrs.___, Indian captive--127
Orahood, Capt. Harper, Colorado Volunteer--177
Otis, George. K, stage line supt.--142
Our Wild Indians--47
Ouray, Ute Chief--2, 71, 73; biog. 68, 69, 70
Padouca. See Comanche Indians
Pawnee Indians--2, 18, 21; history, 18, 19, 20, 22
Pigeon's Ranch, N. Mex.--118
Pike, Lt. Zebulon--13, 20, 21, 44, 48

Pike's Peak--31, 44, 49, 57, 59
Platte Cañon--14, 44
Point of Rocks, Indian camp--88, 90
Powder Face, Indian Chief--148
Pueblo Indians--2, 3
Purgatoire River--141
Pursley, James, early explorer--13
Quartelejo, Pueblo Indian outpost--3, 4
Raven's son, Arapahoe warrior--148, 149
Republican River, Indian camps--19, 21, 47, 229
Robbins boys, killed by Indians--210-11, 212, 214
Robbins, Capt. S. M. at Indian council--169
Roman Nose, Cheyenne Chief--148, 223
Roper, Laura, Indian captive--127
Ruxton, Lt. George F., British explorer, cited--35-37, 38-42, 44, 45-46
Sage, Rufus B., author--30, 37, 44
Sand Creek battle--101-13, 156-58, 160-64, 166-69, 175, 177, 178; weather during, 95, 96, 113
Sand Creek battle investigations. See Congressional Committee, investigations; Committee on

the Conduct of War, investigations
Sargent, Nelson, at Indian councils--169
Sayre, Maj.___, Colorado Volunteer--166, 177
Scidmore, Miss___, author--7
Shawnee Indians--10
Sheridan Gen. Philip H., Indian policy--185-86, 190
Sherman, Gen. Wm. T., refuses help--226-28
Shooks Run, Indian raid--210, 210
Shoshone Indians--5, 7, 9
Shoup, Col. George L., Colorado Volunteer--94, 98, 122, 161, 173; at Indian council, 148; testimony, Sand Creek battle, investigations, 166-71, 172
Simpson party, pursues Indians --195, 200-02, 215
Sioux Indians--2, 7, 9, 12, 13, 14, 19, 47-65 *passim*, 126, 127, 128, dwellings, 23, 24; enemies of Utes, 69; history, 17, 18; as hostiles, 162, 164, 228, 229; plan war on settlers, 131, 136, 138
Slough, Col. John P., Colorado Volunteer--117
Smith, J. Bright, at Indian council--169
Smith, John, interpreter--169
Smith, Ren, pursues Indians-- 79

Smoky Hill River, Indian camp --101, 111, 112, 125, 151, 173, 229
Smoky Hill wagon road--64, 201, 22
Snyder, Mrs.___, Indian captive--127
Soule, Capt.___--119, 120, 121
South Park: described--8, 36, 42, 49; Indian wars in, 53, 54, 55, 58
Spanish expeditions against Indians--4, 6, 9, 19-21, 28
Stage coaches, attacked by Indians--93-94, 115
Steck, Amos, at Indian council --169
Sumner, Col. E.V., Indian fighter--17
Taos lightning, and Indians-- 68
Tallman, Jonathan, killed by Indian--220
Talbert, Job, killed by Indians --200
Tappan, Lt. Col. Samuel F., Colorado Volunteer--117, 119, 120, 122
Teachout, H.M., and hostiles --194, 197, 198, 199, 216
Teller, Sen. H.M., Colorado Volunteer--177
Templeton, Lt. A.J., Colorado Volunteer--95, 222, 224
Third Regiment of Colorado Volunteers--94, 95-99, 115, 116,

121, 122, 160, 161, 176, 177; in
Sand Creek battle, 101-13;
mustered out, 113
Tyler, Capt., Colorado
Volunteer--144, 171
U.S. Bureau of Indian Affairs
--120, 135, 136, 137, 145, 179,
189, 193; policies questioned,
179-80, 183, 184
U.S. War Department, ignores
requests for help--137, 144,
228, 230
Ute Indians--4, 35, 50, 52, 71,
72, 73, 131, 192; description
of, 7, 8; dwellings, 23, 24;
friendly with settlers, 68-
74; history, 5, 6, 9, 10; wars
with plains Indians, 17, 18,
25, 26, 46, 53, 54, 56, 57, 58,
65-67, 75, 83, 229. *See also*
White River Utes
Ute Pass--13, 46, 47, 53, 58, 75,
191, 194
Villazur, Lt. Col., Spanish
officer--20

Wagon-trains--16, 75, 154, 155
Wanless, Capt. John, at
Indian council--169
War Bonnet, Cheyenne Chief--
152
Whirlwind, Indian--148
White Antelope, Cheyenne
Chief--128, 133, 149; friendly
to settlers, 125, 127, 134; at
Indian councils, 169
Whitley, ___, Indian agent--148
"Wild Bill", early settler--
195, 203
Whiteley, Maj. ___, at Indian
council--169
Wilson, Lt. Luther, Colorado
Volunteer--160, 168
Wolf, John, Colorado
Volunteer--95
Wynkoop, Maj. E.W.--119,
120, 125, 126, 128, 133, 134,
150, 186; at Indian council,
169; letter, 130; testimony,
Sand Creek investigations,
121; with Indian Bureau, 189